THE Time Bandit™

STRUCTURED TIME & WORKFLOW

Solution

EDWARD G. BROWN

COHEN BROWN PICTURE COMPANY
LOS ANGELES, CALIFORNIA

W

Published by

Cohen Brown Picture Company
Los Angeles, CA
www.cohenbrown.com

Distributed by Greenleaf Book Group LLC

For ordering information or special discounts for bulk purchases,
please contact Greenleaf Book Group LLC,
PO Box 91869, Austin, TX 78709, 512.891.6100.

Design by Stan Hulen
Hulen Graphics & Design, Dallas, TX
www.hulendesign.com

Illustrations by Ray Harris
RayHarrisStudio.com
and
David Legaspi

Library of Congress Control Number: 2013955198

Hardcover ISBN 13: 978-0-9899151-1-3
Paperback ISBN 13: 978-0-9899151-0-6

Printed in the United States of America on acid-free paper

14 15 16 17 18 19   10 9 8 7 6 5 4 3 2 1

First Edition

Thanks

Dedication

This book, and every happy moment I had writing it, I dedicate to my precious family – Shari, Neda, Derek, Ardeshir, Shaudee and Rhoda – whose belief in me has always shored up mine when it faltered, and from whose talents and wisdom I draw daily inspiration. I started this book because of my own faith; I finished it because of theirs.

Acknowledgments

With my deepest appreciation
to so many for proving once again
that "no man is an island."

Acknowledgments must begin with thanking God for my wife **Shari,** who has led me to the life I strove to have but would never have without her. I would still be searching the world for the benefits of Quiet Time, instead of finding them within, where she taught me I would. As this book unfolded, her wise counsel (and even wiser economizing of it) gave me courage to make disclosures I never expected to make (see especially the deeply traumatized five-year-old), but without which the book would have been a poorer thing.

And my "children" – my daughter **Neda** and her husband **Ardeshir** (and my granddaughter **Shaudee**, the 3-year-old chairman of the board) and my son **Derek**. I am not the first man to wonder, *"I wrought this?"* when seeing offspring making their own brilliance in this vast world that we only pretend to prepare them for. They all gave me advice and ideas for this book, sometimes in the form of casual remarks astounding for their accuracy. If they bring the same cool objectivity to their own pursuits, I have no fears for them.

My big sister, **Rhoda Irwin,** who, when she read an early, short passage from my book, promptly did as she has done all my life – criticized it with wonderful input that I actually used (thanks, Sis!) and praised me as only sisters can do.

Then to **Ruben Rubinstein** who probably didn't know, when he joined me as a very young man as our first Chief Financial Officer, that one of his most important attributes would turn out to be courage. First, the courage to rise to whatever new

CONTINUED ON THE NEXT PAGE

job our frenetically entrepreneurial company added to his description – counselor, trainer, consultant, and suddenly, editor. And second, the courage to challenge me. Whenever I need to be talked out of a firmly held intention (as mine usually are) everybody gives the job to Ruben. Without a doubt, his courage to challenge has created a better book, if a grayer Ruben.

And to **Ann Cain** who does for me on the written page what singers do for songwriters. With the apt analogy, anecdote, interjection, or other "Ann-Cain-ism," she helped Ruben make my story come alive and bring my insights closer to my readers. And for proving once again that a good collaboration includes people with whom one's first inclination is often to disagree and ultimately to collude.

Chris Phillips, nominally my personal assistant for many years, but, in truth, Focal Locking personified; he is the man whose patience with my Type-B-isms, respect for clock and calendar, and kind intercession between me and my cherished Time Bandits made it possible for this book to be completed at all. More than that, Chris became my quiet critic and seamless interpreter, anticipating Ruben's and Ann's criticisms, and making the book-writing experience happier for all of us.

In the book's art director, **Stan Hulen,** I found not only a brilliant counterpart for my writing, sensitive to my wishes and working with a swift certainty rare in an artist, but also a Quiet Time soulmate. It was Stan's epiphany about alone time, similar to mine, that fueled his distinguished career as surely as his work makes the book a delight to the eye.

As for the book's illustrator, I refer to **Ray Harris** as "my paintbrush." So talented and skillful is he that when I am still floundering for words to describe a desired image, over his shoulder I see it materialize on his computer screen, with wit and wisdom embedded in every detail, and then I see what I meant to say.

Essential if less visible in this book's creation are the members of **The Cohen Brown Management Group**. Each brings valuable, individual strength, intelligence and the feedback to our business so often and seamlessly that it is impossible to demark their many contributions to the book.

Those are the people who helped make this book a reality, but before them came those who also deserve acknowledgement, though they were long gone before pen met paper. My parents, **William and Rachel Brown,** who, despite any of my decisions, always had steadfast faith no matter what. **Don Ho,** my longtime friend and partner, whose example, great and otherwise, helped form the kind of leader I became....

Preface

We have all been guilty of stealing time from those around us by interrupting them when they are trying to get something done.

Did you
know that's
you
on the cover?

Don't be offended, it's me, too.

You are somebody's Time Bandit. We all are.

We have all been guilty of stealing time from those around us by interrupting them when they are trying to get something done.

Bandits wear masks to disguise themselves, and Time Bandits wear the most innocent disguises. They come as our friends, our family, our co-workers, our customers, our bosses.

They are so innocent of intent – the one on the cover has a winning little smile, doesn't he? He doesn't intend to steal from you. But if he interrupts you while you are trying to get something done, steal from you he does.

Time Bandits steal your precious time, and what are you going to do about it? Oh, I know there are those books that will tell you to "Just Say No!" when your Time Bandits interrupt you, but "Just Say No!" could be very self-destructive. So, to avoid insulting them, how do you get the benefits of "no" without saying "NO!"?

This book will not only tell you *what* to do, with "executional excellence," it also explains *how*. Without all of the "what to do" and "how to do it" lessons and skills in this book, you will remain forever at the mercy of your nice, smiling Time Bandits. This book teaches you *how* to put an end to unwanted, unnecessary, and unproductive interruptions that steal your time.

So look at it this way: if you were hoping to find a typical time management book, with another list of time-saving tips, or another way to chart time, or more disciplines to impose on your stressed-out self, you have the wrong book. Books like that already fill the bookshelves of those who are just as time-starved and distressed as they were before they read them.

The Time Bandit Solution is, in contrast, a *how-to* book that draws on sociology, psychology, management theory, humor, and a lifetime of experience to arm you with all the communication arts and skills techniques, scripts, and plans it takes to negotiate with your Time Bandits, overcome their objections, secure their cooperation, get back your time, and use it well. In other words, it will develop your interpersonal relationship management skills. What a Triple Crown! You create better relationships, they get your undivided attention, and you get your stolen time back!

It's all here, between the covers of this book. Every chapter will take you that much closer to actually doing what you have long vowed to do: find the time you need to do all the things you want to do. When you finish this book, you will have that time, and you will know how to use it to make your life better. And if I'm wrong, I'll provide you with a 100% "misery-back guarantee!"

This book teaches you how to **put an end to unwanted, unnecessary, and unproductive interruptions** that steal your time.

What's inside

The Time Bandit Solution is divided into three sections depicted in our conceptual model below. The matrix on the right will serve as a table of contents by describing the content of each chapter.

START HERE

III
Time Gained
Behaviorial
Planning

I
Time Loss
Interruption
Issues

II
Time Loss
Interruption
Solutions

The Time Bandit Solution

Intro

The Sands of Time

*Lives of great men
all remind us,
We can make
our lives sublime
And, departing,
leave behind us
Footprints on the
sands of time.*

— HENRY WADSWORTH
LONGFELLOW,
"A PSALM OF LIFE"

**I wrote this self-help book
to save my own life.** Not literally; my
death wasn't imminent. But I *was* watching
precious years, months, days, and hours slip
away without being able to accomplish all that I
wanted to. I was desperate for more time.

Then I realized that I already had the solution.
I had already cracked the code for how to
create more time. I had been doing it
subconsciously at various stressful points in
my career. I just hadn't thought of it that
way. And I hadn't thought of applying the
secret to the rest of my life – to making my
remaining years more fruitful, less frantic,
and more satisfying.

So when I felt the fleetness of time stealing joy from my life,
I recalled what I had learned the hard way during my multiple careers
across many decades. I am living testimony that "a man who loves
what he does isn't truly working." My entrepreneurial pursuits were all
over the map. With great partners, I founded and
ran companies that managed
Hollywood stars, television shows
and athletes, leased heavy equipment, owned nightclubs and restaurants, provided e-learning tools,
and wrote and produced music.

In 1979, with my current partner
Martin L. Cohen, MD, I co-founded
the Cohen Brown Management
Group to provide consulting services,
sales training, and behavioral change
management in the financial services

**Marty Cohen
(below left) and
Edward Brown**

industry. Marty and I have written, produced, and are featured in dozens of video-based training programs that have changed the lives of their participants and the fortunes of their companies.

When I write that the lessons of *The Time Bandit Solution* can change *your* life, I am drawing on decades of on-the-ground, practical experience. AND I am drawing on the most personal of experiences – a new lease on my own life in the form of more time – to help you do for yourself what I did for myself.

Because my partners and I ran our companies lean, I always had a wide variety of duties: strategy, business development, funding, artist management, finance, consulting, recruiting, coaching, writing curricula, administration – you name it. I honestly enjoyed these different duties, but when they all rolled onto my desk at the same time, or when I was interrupted in one domain to take on another, I couldn't do any of them justice.

I was living a career that begged for great time management, but I was a poor time manager. I *wanted* to be good at it. I wanted to give myself freely to all my clients, to mentor and to learn from the people I hired, to be a devoted husband and father, and to refresh myself with leisurely pursuits. But even working 12 and 14 hour days, I still found myself coming up short, annoying a client, disappointing colleagues, being late for dinner, and too stressed to enjoy leisure. I was unhappy.

I began to feel that I was over promising and under performing my "wannabe" service, business, social, and parental commitments. Finally, I hit an emotional and psychological wall going 80 miles a second and declared, *"Enough is enough."*

I eventually came up with a solution-based epiphany that manifested from the following question: *"Ed, when were you the most productive?"* I realized it was when overwhelming distress about competing work priorities in my various careers drove me to duck into what I called **"Quiet Time."**

Here's how the Quiet Time solution worked: when I absolutely, positively had to get something done, but was prevented from doing it by the press of multiple and varied duties, I would physically and mentally subtract myself from the rest of the world until that obligation was completed. No distractions, no interruptions, no multi-tasking until I had cleared the deck and was sure that I had taken the time and given proper consideration to any decision that needed to be made and the possible resultant outcomes.

When I write that **the lessons of *The Time Bandit Solution* can change your life,** I am drawing on decades of on-the-ground, practical experience. AND I am drawing on the most personal of experiences **– a new lease on my own life in the form of more time –** to help you do for yourself what I did for myself.

Overwhelming distress about competing work priorities in my various careers drove me to duck into what I called **Quiet Time.**

So I decided to delve further into how and why my Quiet Time experiences were so powerful, and if and how I could develop Quiet Time into a process-driven lifestyle versus a one-off, now and then event. As I endeavored to expand the repetition of Quiet Time, from now and then, to a monthly, weekly, and daily process, I formalized, internalized, and embedded Quiet Time such that it would become woven into the behavioral tapestry and DNA of my day-to-day life.

Eventually, Quiet Time evolved into a new time-management problem-solving process entitled "Time Locking." I define Time Locking as knowing how to carve out disciplined and focused set periods of time, just the right length for the job at hand and at the appropriate time of day, week, month, or year during which the time locker is totally uninterruptible except for bona fide emergencies. I then ran into my first predictable challenge:

How would I convey my unavailability to people accustomed to finding me with an open door, delighted to show my respect and pleasure by dropping everything for them? Suddenly appearing selfish or unresponsive simply would not work. I needed a way of explaining how and why Time Locking would make more valuable the time I *did* spend with them. If I could control my Time Bandits, I would rightfully restore all the time that had been inadvertently stolen by them.

After all, our Time Bandits aren't strangers on the street or wrong numbers on the phone. They are our most treasured relationships: clients, colleagues, family, and friends.

I eventually realized that the answer was to artfully explain to the Time Bandits that Time Locking was as good for them as it was for me utilizing a pre-scripted and rehearsed request for the Time Bandits' indulgence. But it went way beyond scripting. It involved knowing the communications arts and skills necessary for persuading, negotiating with, and/or selling the Time Bandits on the mutual benefits of Time Locking.

Having analyzed and resolved the cause and effect of my own time-management challenges, I then observed the behavior of others, and interviewed scores of people from all different walks of life and executives at all levels. They were largely unanimous in their response. Their complaints about time matched mine, but I discerned an important subtext: they *said* they lacked enough time, but what I was listening to was a litany about their interruptions. I heard the truth – they lacked *control* over their time.

I'll never forget that moment of discovery – I felt like Archimedes in the bathtub or Newton under the apple tree! *"Eureka! They, like me, have too many interruptions!"*

Although prioritization, planning, and being structured is crucially important (and will be discussed later in *The Time Bandit Solution),* the answer for them, as it was for me, was the subject that no one seemed to want to talk or write about. The key was not to work harder but instead to work smarter by controlling the killer of time, the bane of our culture, the thief of precious time – *interruptions.*

Interruptions treat that treasured, finite resource like the cheapest of commodities. Worse, when I look around at my Time Bandits, I see people who believe themselves powerless to change the dynamic – to take back *their* time, attend to their *own* priorities, and relieve the stress of powerlessly watching time slip away. They don't realize that interruptions are thieves – they think they must tolerate the depredations of each interruption.

It became crystal clear to me that as a change management specialist, it would not only be my privilege but indeed my obligation to help others do for themselves what I had done for myself – arrest this predator of time, because if we don't control interruptions we can't control our time. And if we don't control our time, frankly, we simply don't control our lives.

Just when I thought I had it all worked out for them as well as for myself, during my own Quiet Time, I was confronted with a new Time Bandit which I dubbed, **"Mental Leakage."** As a result of Mental Leakage, and the loss of concentration and focus it creates, I came to realize that our most invidious, stubborn, and uncooperative Time Bandit was sometimes ourselves.

As full-fledged creatures of a culture of interruptions, thriving on controlled chaos and multi-tasking, we are likely to be our own worst enemies of our own **Time Locks.** So, I asked myself, how to make sure I really used my Time Locks to concentrate on a single goal and complete it? How to let the uninterrupted period feel like a gift not to be squandered by daydreaming? How not to keep one of my ears cocked for the ringing phones or the visitor needing "just a minute or two"?

The key was not to work harder but instead to **work smarter by controlling the killer of time,** the bane of our culture, the thief of precious time – **interruptions.**

The solution was **Focal Locking,** which, once conceived, had to be defined, codified, and practiced, practiced, practiced as diligently as any new skill. So I did that, using myself as my first student. I learned how to make my precious Time Locking sessions productive, peaceful, and sometimes even joyous. I investigated the latest in neuroscience and its relationship to our interruption culture and interruption addiction. I studied mental relaxation techniques and visualization exercises to create a hospitable environment for the ability to focus sharply. I devised tactics to keep me on task during my Time Locks.

These days, my time is filled with purpose and mostly devoid of distress about time. I won't claim I never succumb to interruptions, after five decades of habitually doing so. But I estimate that, week to week, I have recovered about 50% to 60% of my stolen time. This is the precious time that used to otherwise slip through my fingers while I thought I was working so wisely. It is an extraordinary gift that I have given myself of increased productivity, closeness to my clients and colleagues, and my own quality of life.

Week to week, I estimate that I have recovered about 50% to 60% of my stolen time.

When the global financial crisis forced layoffs at many of our client companies, and the lament about "not enough time" became more vociferous and widespread, I recognized that my hard-won knowledge could help a lot of people. So I used my training and teaching skills to share it with business people I knew who were, like me, desperate for more time. I created a course for businesses called **Structured Time and Workflow Management (STWM).** Even the most skeptical of the executives who took the course became enthusiastic converts when STWM changed their lives.

One of our most fervent converts talks about STWM's gift almost spiritually. He says, *"There are two ways you can stretch your life: adding extra years, or getting more out of life every day. With this program our people are learning to get more out of life every day – not just at work but in how they live their lives."*

Time and again I heard, *"Ed, this is extraordinary. You should write a book about it."* So I did.

Now, within your hands, as with the thousands who have attended STWM, you have what changed those lives – *The Time Bandit Solution (TBS).*

In it you will find the tools for gaining control of your time and, ultimately, your life.

Here's what to expect as you read this book:
- Chapters 1:00 through 3:00 zero in on the issue of interruptions – why we have them, why we tolerate them, why they are so persistent.

- When you get to Chapters 4:00 through 7:00 you will see the doors opening to practical solutions. There you will come to believe that you can actually solve the issues that seemed so entrenched at first.
- Finally, in Chapters 8:00 through 12:30, I will help you make the most of this new and valuable resource on your hands – this surplus time that can make better lives for you, your colleagues, and others in your life.

Who should read this book? The people who can best profit from the lessons of this book are these:

- A member of the corporate world, no matter whether your industry and profession is in diversified financial services, health care, telecommunications, hospitality, manufacturing, or distribution, who, despite the inestimable, spiraling-down economic ravages that result in severe downsizing and hiring freezes, insists upon sustained productivity peak performance.
- All professionals who recognize interruptions as the quintessential cause for loss of billable time. They are lawyers, accountants, consultants, business managers, medical doctors. These professionals regularly hear interruptive, time-consuming, wasteful questions such as these:

  "I had my tax return prepared by an accountant, but would you mind taking a look and telling me if he did a good job?"

  Or:

  "Dr. Smith, I know you're not my doctor, but I have some medical issues, and I'd very much appreciate your second opinion."
- Anyone who has already tried working harder, working smarter, working longer hours, and still can't find enough time.
- Anyone whose day is filled with unwanted, unnecessary, and unproductive interruptions but feels powerless to resist them.
- Anyone who manages, parents, or teaches people like those described above.

Throughout my 37 years of teaching and training, I have come to realize that, in order to sustain behavioral and educational knowledge transfer, a certain amount of repetition is required. Therefore, please bear with me when I pre-position the next chapter by stating the key elements of the prior chapter. This concept is called the "Gazinta Principle" and enables the reader to better connect the chapters that are designed to be interdependent on one another, and to remember where he left off regardless of whether or not he has put down the book.

I hope this book does for you what it did for me and what STWM does for our participants: I hope it restores your precious time back to its rightful owner.

Now, within your hands, as with the thousands who have attended STWM, **you have what changed those lives** – *The Time Bandit Solution.*

Time Loss Interruption Issues

In the Time Loss Interruption Issues section, we will identify the causes, effects, and the reasons of major time management issues, as well as addressing the distress caused by the feeling of being overwhelmed with too much to do and not enough time to do it in.

™

Lucy gives us an intimate look at how **a person starts out trying to do a good job** and then slowly but surely loses her dignity trying to do the impossible. That's pathos, and **it's only Lucy's comedic talent that makes that pathos funny.**

"Speed It Up, Boys!"

It has to be one of the funniest sketches ever. A dozen times I've watched Lucy in the chocolate factory, and I still laugh. The faster the production line goes, the more chocolates she stuffs in her mouth, blouse, and hat. The supervisor checks in and, finding a clear conveyor belt, compliments Lucy, then shouts, *"Speed it up, boys!"* while the camera gives us a close-up of Lucy's horrified face.

I happened to see the sketch again during a period when I was carrying on a respectful argument with a top executive at one of our client companies. We had trained hundreds of his people on sales and service. Now, due to failures in other parts of the company, he was making massive cuts to sales and service staff. Naturally, he was keeping sales and service goals almost as high!

The managers and employees **left behind to pick up the work-load** of thousands of laid-off colleagues, already stressed, stretched, and buffeted by constant change before the layoffs, now face Sisyphean odds.

It was blindingly evident to me that he was making a colossal mistake asking them to do more with less without providing his people with a methodology for obtaining those goals. Good sales and service practices don't take more time than bad ones, but they do take time, and he wasn't claiming his people had time on their hands before the layoffs. Instead his rationale seemed to be, "We all have to do more with less. We all have to adapt." Necessity as a strategy, if you will.

Lucy proved how well that works. She gives us an intimate look at how a person starts out trying to do a good job and then slowly but surely loses her dignity trying to do the impossible. That's pathos, and it's only Lucy's comedic talent that makes that pathos funny.

But in the real world, pathos stays pathos – it doesn't get funny. It ruins the work environment. It kills morale, productivity, and profits.

So why is Lucy in the chocolate factory relevant today? Because of the socioeconomic devastation that occurs with every downturn or financial crisis and, despite the usually slow recoveries, budgets remain frozen and workforces continue to be slashed. Let's take a look at some examples of these massive layoffs from this last decade alone: American Airlines 13,000, Dallas Independent School District 12,000–15,000, T-Mobile 1,900, Tennessee Valley Authority 1,000, J. C. Penney thousands, Bank of America 30,000, Hostess (the cupcake company) 18,000. Smaller companies have slashed in proportionate numbers. Overtime hours are commonplace.

Now consider that the workforces left in these companies still have to keep the company running and running well. These managers and employees left behind to pick up the workload of thousands of laid-off colleagues, already stressed, stretched, and buffeted by constant change before the layoffs, now face Sisyphean odds. Management keeps their goals unrelentingly high – for quality service, new revenue, higher productivity, better innovation, perfect compliance, surer safety, and tighter security.

And now they have to do it with fewer people.

How will they do it? Technology can sometimes help, but the essential work of any company – forming relationships, understanding customers, producing more, and making wise decisions – is still done by humans with two hands, one head, and must be squeezed into eight or so hours a day. When management has wrung all the sweat equity it can from the employees, and they are taxed beyond their ability to work well, their work suffers, along with their job satisfaction and, ultimately, customer satisfaction.

"Too much work and not enough time" is the perfect motto for lowering morale, losing customers as well as employees, shrinking sales, and decimating profits.

So in today's downsized business world, legions of proud professionals are "doing a Lucy" every day, scrambling to do their jobs when they have no chance of succeeding because they do not have the time.

This book can't affect the layoffs. But it can and does show these proud professionals where their time has gone, and how they can get it back. It will show them how to recapture the time stolen by our culture of distractions and interruptions and, ultimately, how to do more with less.

Time, especially in this period of rampant layoffs, is as precious as water in the midst of a drought. They say time is money, and maybe it is – we all know what is meant by that. But time is a lot more than money. It's how we measure out our lives. Our lifetimes. The time of our lives.

When management has wrung all the sweat equity it can from the employees, and they are taxed beyond their ability to work well, their work suffers, along with their job satisfaction and, ultimately, customer satisfaction.

With reduced staff, **wasting time at work** is unconscionable – that's why we all feel so guilty when we find ourselves doing just that, unwillingly, unintentionally, but definitely doing it.

With reduced staff, wasting time at work is unconscionable – that's why we all feel so guilty when we find ourselves doing just that, unwillingly, unintentionally, but definitely doing it. Imagine knowing that you could change this behavioral phenomenon – that you would never again waste time against your will.

In the subsequent chapters I will demonstrate to you how. And I will illustrate for you how better time management is good for more than productivity – it builds self-confidence, self-esteem, job satisfaction (just as its absence in the chocolate factory made Lucy miserable) and it engenders gratitude from clients and colleagues.

Okay, "Speed it up, boys!"

Too Much to Do

"We have too much to do, and not enough time to do it!" Does this sound familiar? It should. This is what, for the past 35 years, many of you have been telling me.

As you know, this has long been the most common workplace lament in the old, let alone today's, economy.

When seeking to analyze this lament with management, what we would very often hear is, *"They're just using time management as an excuse."* In economic downturns marked by layoffs, hiring freezes, and tighter deadlines, the lament was no longer considered just an excuse, but rather a reason for underperformance. And yet the echoes of apathetic managers, completely ignoring the complaints as if speaking about the weather, masked their own desperation, *"Okay, Okay, I know you're too busy. Well, join the club. Now let's talk about something we CAN change."*

Having too much to do and not enough time to do it must be understood as a **danger signal** – one that can **destroy a company** just as surely as an untreated illness can eventually kill its victim.

It didn't
take long for
**the layoff
"survivors"**
– these highly-
trained, highly
accomplished
performers –
to object.

But like a nagging pain, having too much to do and not enough time to do it must be understood as a danger signal – one that, when ignored and combined with economic downturns, can destroy a company just as surely as an untreated illness can eventually kill its victim.

I know this because I saw it happen, and it was like a death in the family because it happened to a client of ours, a bank in the northeast of the United States.

This bank was one of North America's most prestigious banks. Its wealth management group had hired my company, Cohen Brown Management Group, to establish the world standard for banking industry sales and service culture among the bank's professionals. This transformation would increase their market share, share of wallet, and customer loyalty – making them "uncatchably first" in their market.

The project began from a position of strength. The bank's wealth management business unit was the single most profitable segment of the bank. Their wealth management specialists controlled about 70% of the bank's most profitable deposits. These specialists were brilliant, ambitious, and well-educated MBAs and PhDs. Their top managers were aggressive – aware that they had to perform at high levels to compete successfully.

They learned quickly from our programs: how to be clear, capable, and motivated; how to execute with excellence, from the front lines to the back office to the executive suite. Everyone was prepared to perform their part of the mission. They worked hard and eventually achieved their customer-centric and revenue-driven goals of establishing the bank's Wealth Management Division as having a world-class (if not world-standard) sales and service culture. In short, they were on their way to being an extraordinary success story.

But then came a modest downturn in the economy – not a recession, just a cyclical dip, not expected to have dreadful or lasting effects. It called for some downsizing, which the bank did.

It didn't take long for the layoff "survivors" – these highly trained, highly accomplished performers – to object. *"But now,"* they said, *"we can't get all of our work done."* It was true. When they had to take on the workloads of their laid-off colleagues, they were pushed beyond their capacities.

What happens when you push a car's engine too hard for the gear it's in? Sadly, that's what management did to this finely tuned team of performers. *It's a great car – it can go faster. It has to.*

And when the engine protested – when the bank's highly educated, highly trained top performers objected, their objections were ignored. Despite the increased workloads, management stubbornly assumed that the chorus of complaints was just a standard lament, "an excuse," not a sign of great workers being forced to "pull a Lucy."

Like Lucy's manager, blind to her chocolate-stuffed mouth, blouse, and hat, choosing instead to "speed it up, boys," the bank's management assumed the complaints would tail off once people got used to the new staffing levels. No doubt management could foresee only one alternative (lower sales goals) and rejected it.

We begged them to listen, to probe – to get to the bottom of this extraordinary chorus of "We have too many accounts."

"These are your star performers! They didn't complain when we put them through tough training. Not when you gave them stretch goals. Not when you stretched them again. These are not whiners," I said, *"please, I ask, let us hear them out."* After all in Wealth Management, I had pointed out, the average account executive servicing millionaires is not asked to handle an account load of more than 60 clients. At this bank it ranged up to 150 accounts despite not having proper time management protocols.

Plus, these people had no assistants to answer phones or placate the 90-year-old heiress who would call them just to have someone to talk to. After all, their policy was to "never offend an inbound caller."

Interruptions had always plagued these top performers, but once layoffs cut deeply into their ranks, **they simply could not get their work done.**

I discerned a common thread, **"My time really isn't my own.** *I have walk-ins; I have call-ins; I have interruption after interruption.* **Others manage my time; I don't."**

Management was unmoved. Regrettably, it all unraveled incredibly fast. The top performers jumped ship, taking their books of business to the competition. Earnings tumbled, shareholders complained, management invested in speculative real estate, and, ultimately, the bank was seized and liquidated. If you research the reason for the bank's failure you will learn that it was because of bad real estate investments. However, by virtue of those employees who suffered along with their clients the everyday trauma of having too much to do and not enough time to do it in, I will always ask myself just how much did the crisis in Wealth Management contribute to its downfall.

I'm not a man to entertain regrets, but I still grieve that I was not able to persuade senior management to take the complaints seriously. If I had, I have no doubt that we would have quickly penetrated the surface complaint about no time. We would have been able to discern the real problem: massive unwanted, unnecessary, and counter-productive interruptions. Interruptions had always plagued these top performers, but once layoffs cut deeply into their ranks, they simply could not get their work done. To them, it looked like too much to do. But perhaps if I knew then what I know now, and we were given the chance to teach them the Time Bandit Solution, at least as it pertained to the bank's Wealth Management destiny, the outcome may have been different.

Following the most recent financial recession, we began hearing echoes of that same lament. We queried our global clientele in the midst of the recent recession when many of them have had hiring freezes or layoffs. They told me, *"Ed, what our people continually tell us is they simply have too much to do, too many inbound and outbound problem-solving calls, too much handholding, too many administrative details, too many compliance details, too much paperwork, too many meetings, too many performance assessments, too many supervisory tasks. Ed, there's simply too much to do and not enough time to do it."*

Similarly, over and over, we were told by managers that these were the complaints of *"underachieving ninjas."*

I did a deep dive analysis into the issues surrounding account overload given realities versus time management excuses.

I had to ask myself, *"After all these years of great success, do our clients have to throw in the towel because of layoffs and hiring freezes? Must they accept diminished performance and disappointment during hard times like today? Or can I find a way to help them increase performance in a downsized company so that the survivors of the downsizing could leverage time such that they magically, if not fundamentally, learn how to do more with less?"*

I probed a little more into our clients' employees' complaints and discerned a common thread, *"My time really isn't my own. I have walk-ins; I have call-ins; I have interruption after interruption. Others manage my time; I don't."*

My revelation from all this research was phenomenal.

On one hand, those front-line staff functionaries (the survivors of downsizing) could not keep up with the demands and management productivity goals. On the other hand, managers, thought of as Time Bandits by their subordinates, were themselves Time Bandit victims.

Now, as then, the pandemic and pervasive cause and effect associated with interruptions has to be resolved.

The solution begins with an admission. We all have to admit employer/employee, client/manager, it makes no difference when it comes to interruptions; we all suffer in our own way equally. We have to admit that our shortage of time occurs more as a result of interruptions than almost anything else.

When we don't control interruptions, **we concede control of our time to whoever or whatever shows up** to claim it. Our lives are not our own to direct.

Anything that disrupts your workflow, no matter the source, **is an interruption.**

The revelation was the discovery that the fundamental issue was not just a shortage of time, but a surplus of interruptions. *"When we don't control interruptions, we concede control of our time to whoever or whatever shows up to claim it. Our lives are not our own to direct."*

The mistake these employees made – their conclusion that they didn't have enough time, was understandable. That's how they experienced the feeling of being overwhelmed and the distress and drain that interruptions caused. After dealing with streams of distractions and interruptions, making them unable to get to their priorities, under the circumstances, it was reasonable for them to conclude that they needed more time for their work. But to me the revelation was both subtle and thunderous: if I could curb their interruptions, they would have the time they needed. So I bored deeper into the plague of interruptions. I learned how to see them not as harmless diversions but as ruinous distractions.

Interruptions steal our time in five insidious ways, which we call **the Five Time-Loss Factors:**

The Five Time-Loss Factors

1. Interruptions
2. Restarts
3. Momentum Loss
4. Do-Overs
5. Distress Manifestations

First, Interruptions. Anything that disrupts your workflow, no matter the source, is an interruption. It might come in the form of a colleague asking your opinion. You take the call, do the research, call the colleague back, convey the answer, and wrap up with various polite phrases. How much time does that whole process take?

Next, Restarts. A restart is the effort involved in getting back to where you left off prior to an interruption. Sometimes it may involve no more than shaking off the interruption, getting back into the previous

frame of mind, recalling the train of thought, and taking up the right tools again. It is the proverbial *"Now where was I?"* question. But sometimes it takes a much greater effort. Maybe the website you were on timed out, or the people you were talking to dispersed, or you forgot the idea you were about to record, or the customer walked away, or the inspiration disappeared. Time and effort are expended to do no more than get you back where you left off – no added value for all that time and effort.

Then, Momentum Loss. Although harder to quantify than time lost due to restarts, time lost due to loss of momentum is just as insidious. Momentum is what you develop provided you are not interrupted when you are doing repetitive tasks. When professionals lose their rhythm, a little talent seeps away, too.

The more we do repetitive tasks without interruption, the more momentum we build. Left uninterrupted our momentum grows and grows, so we get faster and faster and more accurate. And just when momentum brings you to the peak of your efficiency, someone knocks on your door, comes to your desk, or calls you on the phone and says: *"Hi, I'm your Time Bandit, here to break your momentum. How am I doing?"*

After the Time Bandit extracts his or her ounce of time, you return to the original task in the hopes of trying to regain your momentum.

After the Time Bandit extracts his or her ounce of time, you return to the original task in the hopes of trying to regain your momentum.

The next big Time-Loss Factor is Do-Overs. Who isn't more likely to make mistakes when they are thrown off course by interruptions and then struggle to regain momentum? It's a perfect environment for poor quality and flat-out errors. There's the time it takes to have someone point out your error, the time to apologize and promise to fix it, the actual rework to make it right, and the resending of the corrected work to wherever it has to go. Do-overs can easily take twice the amount of time as doing it right the first time.

Finally, Distress Manifestations. Interruptions create distress, and it shows up in many ways. These manifestations may be subjective, varying significantly from person to person, but they do exist, and they are harmful. The symptoms can vary, too: mental fatigue, irritability, loss of concentration, reduced efficiency, reduced productivity. We will return to this subject later.

In the meantime, let's see if what I have described is relevant to you. Let's review if very much of your time is indeed squandered away to unnecessary interruptions. I would like you to do the following exercise, and hope that you will be as astounded by the results as I was.

Interruptions Quiz

Just before you leave your workplace, write down all the interruptions you faced during the day. Be specific and ask the following questions:

1. **What prevented you** from meeting your deadlines with increased productivity, accuracy, and overall timeliness?

2. **Identify the sources** of the biggest interruptions:
   - Customers
   - Colleagues
   - Supervisors
   - Subordinates
   - Emails
   - Text messages
   - Phone calls
   - Unscheduled meetings

3. **Record** the following information on the Time-Wasted Calculations Worksheet.

	NUMBER	AVG. MIN.	DAILY TOTAL
INTERRUPTIONS			
RESTARTS			
INEFFICIENCIES			
TOTAL			

4. **Estimate the number of interruptions** you have on a typical day and the average time, in minutes, you devote to each interruption.

5. **Estimate the number of restarts** after the interruptions and the average time lost due to each restart.

6. **Estimate how much time you lose** on average due to momentum losses, do-overs, and/or quality-control issues and distress manifestations otherwise known as "inefficiencies."

7. **Calculate your personal daily averages** and total your results to see how much time you believe is devoted to interruptions and stolen by your Time Bandits each week.

It is a large number, isn't it? When we do this in our Structured Time and Workflow Management (STWM) classes, it's never minutes a day, it is *hours*.

Now, talk to some of your colleagues at work about your estimates and see if you can get them to do the same thing.

I believe you'll find that not only are your estimates similar but that the amount of time consumed by interruptions and their wake, when added up among all of you, is a staggering number.

Think about how much time you would save if you didn't have those interruption-related Time-Loss Factors. Given the level of workload and various projects all of you have to complete each week, think of what you could accomplish, individually as well as collectively, if you had all that time back.

Here are some typical averaged-out results from our STWM program presented to the financial services industry; how do yours compare?

- Time Loss from Interruptions   = **238** Minutes per day
- Time Loss from Restarts   =   **84** Minutes per day
- Time Loss from Inefficiencies   =   **50** Minutes per day.

Inefficiencies comprise momentum losses, do-overs, and distress.

All of these averages we've compiled from our STWM classes work out to an estimated 372 minutes. That's 6.2 hours every day, or 31 hours a week! Thirty-one hours a week consumed by the five Time-Loss Factors we've identified. That's almost a whole person!

Naturally, these results will vary from industry to industry, but if your loss-of-time calculations are like those of our clients, **you're typically wasting between 40 to 60 percent of your daily, weekly, monthly, and yearly time.** You're giving about half of your time away as if it were unlimited instead of one of your scarcest resources. Even if your calculations come out different from ours, can you see the value of having just one hour per day returned to you? What could you accomplish in five extra hours per week?

If you simply eliminated these Time-Loss Factors by controlling interruptions, you could, **without working a single extra hour,** gain almost an entire week every month. But if you ignore them – continue to tolerate interruptions – you not only waste your valuable time, but the effects on your company could be disastrous: burnt-out employees, corporate goals unmet, stellar careers destroyed, and millions of dollars of value accumulated over years erased by something that you could control.

If your loss-of-time calculations are like those of other clients, **you're typically wasting between 40 to 60 percent of your time.**

An accounting firm with 1,000 accountants who can recover two hours a day from the time that had been stolen by their Time Bandits now can use the time for productive billing.

Let's convert that to a positive: if you were to eliminate interruptions at your company, what would be the monetary benefits?

A chief analyst, Jonathan B. Spira, wrote an article called "The Cost of Not Paying Attention" wherein he states that *"Interruptions now consume 28% of a knowledge worker's day … Assuming an average salary of $21/hour for a knowledge worker, the cost to business [in the US alone] is $588 billion."* *

These examples illustrate how you might calculate the opportunity for your own company.

● **An accounting firm** with 1,000 accountants who can recover two hours a day from the time that had been stolen by their Time Bandits now can use the time for productive billing. At an average billable rate of $250 an hour, that extra two hours a day would produce **$130 million in incremental revenues a year.**

● **At a consumer goods company,** an extra two hours per day allows a product to be brought to market six months faster without the need for additional personnel. Besides the clear

* Spira, Jonathan B. & Joshua B. Feintuch. "The Cost of Not Paying Attention: How Interruptions Impact Knowledge Worker Productivity." 2005 September. Basex. http://iorgforum.org/wp-content/uploads/2011/06/CostOfNotPayingAttention.BasexReport.pdf

competitive advantage of having a product earlier, the fact that the product is now "on the shelves" six months earlier can produce incremental sales. At an average of 40 sales per day at a rate of $1,250 per unit, the early marketing produces **an incremental $9 million for the company.**

● **Increasingly, technology, construction and engineering companies** are contractually penalized for missing project milestones and deadlines, and for quality and performance problems. If rampant interruptions cause delays in your projects, or contribute to errors that force you to do rework, those penalties and the cost of the rework come straight out of your bottom line. These fines can run into thousands, even millions of dollars, depending on the inconvenience to the public or the cost to the company commissioning the project.

So now the question is, **why?** Why do you and I and everybody else permit such profligate squandering of time when we all know our time is precious and wish that we had more of it? Why would we persist in something that now sounds so self-destructive?

Read on.

Why do you and I and everybody else permit **such profligate squandering of time** when we all know our time is precious and wish that we had more of it?

CHAPTER

2:00

The Interruption Culture

Like most people, I started out as an interrupter, with my mother often admonishing me for it. I wasn't a disobedient child, but anybody could tell, from the boring topics adults nattered on about, that they could use a little diversion, and I was willing. But eventually, like everybody else (except talk show hosts) I got the message and stopped interrupting adults in mid-sentence.

But then as an adult myself, without quite being aware of it, I adopted an interruption habit that for some reason is condoned or at least imitated by virtually all the adults I've ever known. I picked up the phone and called another adult any time I wanted to. They picked up the phone and called me at their convenience. They

I adopted an interruption habit that for some reason is condoned or at least imitated by virtually all the adults I've ever known.

strolled into my office to talk when it pleased them. I did the same, sticking my head in when and where it suited me. We interrupted each other constantly, habitually, remorselessly.

Where was my mother when we needed her!

Now, after my experience at the northeastern US bank and similar situations, I'm death on interruptions again. But it's important to understand why they so pervade our lives before we have any hope of controlling them. That is the purpose of this chapter.

"Interruption Culture?" When I heard that term a couple of years ago, I recognized it for the oxymoron it is. For heaven's sake, what could be less cultured than imposing the impulse of the moment on otherwise engaged adults?

But it's true! We live in a culture where our time is rarely our own, where Quiet Time is mistaken for idleness, and interruptions no long carry the taint of rudeness or rupture.

Even **Winston Churchill** was once quoted as saying, *"Don't interrupt me while I'm interrupting."*

Some blame the interruption culture on the internet era. If you're on the internet and find yourself bored in the slightest, you can, with nothing more than the flick of a finger, distract yourself all around the world, on any subject, in any language, with your audio up or down. You don't have to get up and find a different book. You don't have to pick up the phone and call anybody.

And if you don't distract yourself, the internet will do it for you with ads, videos, or suggestions thrust across the screen at random intervals. Thanks to the infinite distractibility of the internet, the most stolid reader can find himself flitting from site to site, topic to topic, like an over-sugared toddler emptying his entire toy box on the middle of the floor.

But let's be honest. The internet didn't invent the interruption culture any more than it invented gambling. People have been indulging in both for a long time, and I'm old enough to have watched the interruption culture thrive for decades.

And even when people bemoan the interruption culture's impact, they don't seem to resist it very sturdily.

"Interruption Culture?" What could be less cultured than imposing the impulse of the moment on otherwise engaged adults?

For example, some managers, even CEOs, tout an "open door" policy. I understand the symbolism of democratic access and the danger of remote leadership, but if your CEO makes thousands of dollars an hour, what business sense does it make to have the disposition of those hours allocated arbitrarily by anybody with a grievance, a lonely moment, or a needy ego?

Sue Shellenbarger in an article for the *Wall Street Journal* writes:

"The big push in office design is forcing co-workers to interact more. Cubicle walls are lower, office doors are no more and communal cafes and snack bars abound.

"Like most grand social experiments, though, open-plan offices bring an unintended downside: pesky, productivity-sapping interruptions.

"The most common disruptions come from co-workers, as tempting as it is to blame email or instant messaging. Face-to-face interruptions account for one-third more intrusions than email or phone calls, which employees feel freer to defer or ignore, according to a 2011 study in the journal Organization Studies.

"Other research published earlier this year links frequent interruptions to higher rates of exhaustion, stress-induced ailments and a doubling of error rates.

"It's easy to turn to a neighbor for, say, tips on how to tweak a spread sheet or where to go for lunch. But such interruptions—which many feel it would be rude to rebuff—nibble away at the ability to stay on task." *

Isn't there a little egotism in subscribing to the interruption culture? If you're unpopular, **you're not inundated with calls or emails.**

Which is not to say that I'm a great model for controlling interruptions, even if I did invent the Time Bandit Solution. When I overhear my assistant greeting a client on the phone, it's all I can do to not jump on the call, no matter what I'm doing. No matter that I've just assembled my team for a meeting and would leave them cooling their heels, or that my assistant has a deft touch with clients and a calendar and will take care of the client very, very well. I have to silence the inner voice that asks, *"Was that an important caller? Am I under-servicing anyone who needs me?"*

Besides, isn't there a little egotism in acquiescing to the interruption culture? If you're popular, people always want a piece of you, right? If you're unpopular, you're not inundated with calls or emails. They don't have people popping in needing their wisdom, their sympathy, their signature, their nearness. Who hasn't heard themselves "brag-griping" about an over-packed calendar, or how many emails they get, or the phone that never stops ringing? I'm over-scheduled, therefore I am important, right?

*Shellenbarger, Sue. "The Biggest Office Interruptions Are..." *Wall Street Journal,* http://online.wsj.com/article/SB10001424127887324123004579057212505053076.html?mod=WSJ_LifeStyle_Lifestyle_5

But just how important are you if whatever you've chosen to do at any given moment is never as important as the impulse of whoever shows up?

To deal sternly with interruptions in my own work, I deliberately began to think of interruptions as *"stealing"* my time. I began to mentally label my interrupters (including me, with my penchant for distracting myself) as **Time Bandits.**

Time Bandits steal our time by popping in and interrupting us at work. Sometimes they are the perpetrators, but sometimes we seek them out unconsciously. Don't tell me you never wearied of a grueling project and strolled down the hall under the pretense of asking a colleague about it. Or let your mind stray to the weather this weekend, or the upcoming basketball game.

The reason that sometimes we unconsciously take our minds off our focus and send it elsewhere is because we may be addicted. We are so shaped by the interruption culture that if we go without being interrupted for a while, we experience the anxiety of a drug addict deprived of his fix. So accustomed are we to being interrupted that an absence of interruption – a sustained period of single-minded focus feels, for some people, punitive – like being sent to solitary. Or maybe we are simply applying the normal human nature of avoidance behavior. Certainly the difficult task at hand is scarier and/or more tedious than the interruption, *"I'll just do it later."*

What else could account for someone (okay, me) who, feeling the pressure of a critical deadline, and knowing very well that taking or making a non-critical call puts the deadline at risk, will nevertheless enthusiastically pick up the phone? That's interruption addiction: *"I must not. I will not. But here I go."*

To be sure, we come by some of this distracted behavior honestly. *"Take a break,"* our parents told us if they saw signs of imminent meltdown during homework. "Recess" came to mean fun and games on the playground, but its original definition is more mundane: *"a temporary cessation of the customary activities of an engagement, occupation, or pursuit"* – although needed and welcomed, pure interruption if there ever was one. Parents and teachers urged us to seek non-academic outlets at school – play an instrument, go

> To be sure, we come by some of this distracted behavior honestly. ***"Take a break,"*** **our parents told us** if they saw signs of imminent meltdown during homework.

Today we are all at the mercy of the single most interrupting device ever – the personal computer and its progeny whether on our desk, in our hand, or embedded in the television, the car, the refrigerator, or even the dog.

out for a sport. In other words, although healthy interruptions, the recreation did embed that it was OK to take your mind off the main thing at hand.

To get into college we were even tested for our ability to stop, skim, and move on. That's what passing the SAT back then (also known as the Scholastic Aptitude Test, required in some US colleges) was about: not concentrating deeply on any one question but giving each about sixty seconds, picking an answer from the choices presented, and moving on. No time for critical thinking in those days; just figure out the trick of the question or skip it.

And today we are all at the mercy of the single most interrupting device ever – the personal computer and its progeny whether on our desk, in our hand, or embedded in the television, the car, the refrigerator, or even the dog.

We are desperately reliant on this technology, but equally desperate to manage it so that it doesn't manage us. We depend on emails, reminders, alerts, and texts to keep us on top of our tasks, but they constantly interrupt the task at hand.

Mobile phones are even worse, especially now that they are "smart" phones. That is, smart enough to distract even the most focused individuals. Phone ringers, alert beeps, and the vibration of an incoming email break our concentration just as surely as any external uproar. Even when we tell ourselves that we're not answering the phone or responding to a beep, the simple fact that the phone is knocking at our concentration door is enough to disrupt our workflow momentum and break our chain of thought.

Like Time Bandits, these electronic-based interruptions may be frustrating, but often they are secretly welcomed. They break up the monotony of a work day. They relieve the weight of a difficult project. They are diversionary. Like kids ready for recess, we race for the relief even when we know better.

So, who is your worst Time Bandit?

The impatient client? The customer with too much time on his hands? The chatty woman in marketing? The compliance guy always checking up on you? Or you – the person intending/ pretending to be concentrating while pining for the next "unavoidable" interruption?

We are our own worst Time Bandits. Deny even this and we display the behaviors of addicts who claim they can stop at any time. They are in denial. Are you?

Are you secretly welcoming interruptions or enduring them? Are you incapable of insulating yourself from interruptions or have you been cultivating your "recess" gene until you can't wait to be interrupted? For most of us, barring firemen and paramedics, interruptions are self-inflicted because we don't protect ourselves from them and head them off at the pass.

Let's face it; our Time Banditry is a manifestation of our interruption addiction. Overcoming this addiction will require behavior change.

Behavior change is no stranger to Cohen Brown. Within the global diversified financial services industry, as change management agents, we have been recognized by our clients and even our peers as #1 in our space.

So why should you listen to me? Am I a professor of time management at a prestigious university? No!

We are our own worst Time Bandits...
Are you secretly welcoming interruptions or enduring them?

If you think
time manage-
ment behavior
change is
difficult in the
corporate
world, it is
a relative
cake walk
compared
to "herding
celebrity
cats" in the
entertainment
industry where
deadlines are
real deadlines,
**when
thousands
of people are
waiting for
the show
to start.**

Instead, I have lived and taught time management within the context of helping major companies, doctors, lawyers, as well as celebrities, increase their results at the same time as better managing their time.

If you think time management behavior change is difficult in the corporate world, it is a relative cake walk compared to "herding celebrity cats" in the entertainment industry where deadlines are real deadlines, when thousands of people are waiting for the show to start.

It's for this reason I'm able to assure you that *The Time Bandit Solution* is, by necessity, as much a book about the psychology of behavior change as it is about any other aspect of time management.

As a condition to positively changing interruption behavior, we must first acknowledge the harmful effects of our interruption culture. We can then overcome interruptions and all the negative things that follow from them by understanding what we are doing and what others are doing to us, how interruptions affect our concentration and personal well-being, how to avoid them and, finally, the precise techniques for overcoming them.

The bottom line is that all of this change management psychotherapeutic breakthrough behavioral embedding "stuff" really works and it has been proven over decades with over a million users. They are not just touchy feely concepts but, instead, everything that you learn here will be immediately applicable to the real-world environment. This means the techniques that you learn in TBS will work as well now as they did in the past, and I am willing to bet my bottom dollar that they will work as well in the next millennia.

I don't mean to sound boastful but it is our historic success with behavior change with STWM that has given me the courage and the conviction that we can completely abrogate the negative aspects of our interruption culture.

In the next chapter let's examine what our culture of interruptions looks like when it plays itself out in a day in the life of a highly motivated, intelligent, and responsive working professional metaphor named "Tommy Wants-to-Please."

As a condition to positively changing interruption behavior, we must first acknowledge the harmful effects of our interruption culture. **We can then overcome interruptions** and all the negative things that follow from them.

CHAPTER
3:00

Some think of Tommy as a little co-dependent – too, too responsive; **too, too anxious to please** everybody, anywhere, at the same time, always.

Meet Tommy Wants-to-Please

Meet Tommy Wants-to-Please of the First Bank of Anywhere. Although Tommy is a manager at one of the bank's larger branches, Tommy could also be a manager at a hotel, airline, or other company; he could be in manufacturing, distributing, or energy; it makes no difference.

Tommy's most recognizable characteristic is that he is a highly reactive, time-management slave. Tommy wants to please everyone at every hour of the day, reacting to any hint that somebody needs or wants something from him. The phone rings and Tommy answers it, ready to respond to any request. An email alert pops up on his screen and Tommy clicks on it and types away his response. Text messages get returned in seconds.

Like the target in a shooting gallery that spins around whenever the laser bullet hits it, Tommy responds to every command. He is a solid citizen of our Interruption Culture.

Some think of Tommy as a little co-dependent – too, too responsive; too, too anxious to please everybody, anywhere, at the same time, always. If you ask Tommy, however, he simply has just too, too much to do and just doesn't have enough time to do it in.

Tommy's manager believes, as Shakespeare might have said, that Tommy is making *"much ado about nothing."* In fact, his manager believes Tommy's time management complaints are the equivalent of making a *"big mountain out of a proverbial molehill."*

"Come on, Tommy," he says, *"cut the moaning. Interruptions, like rush hour traffic, are a part of life."*

Was the manager right? Must interruptions leave chaos and dysfunction in their wake? These are good questions. Let's look at a typical day in Tommy's life:

8:30 a.m.
After a great weekend, Tommy is full of energy and optimism, enthused to be back at work. The first thing on his to-do list is an important but not difficult Administrative, Operations, and Compliance task – let's call it his AOC Project. It should take about two hours.

Tommy's manager believes, as Shakespeare might have said, that Tommy is making **"much ado about nothing."**

The client only spends 15 minutes and leaves. Just as Tommy begins to regain some lost momentum, **a call comes in from his boss.**

8:40 a.m.
An unexpected client walks in to his office.

The client only spends 15 minutes and leaves. Just as Tommy begins to regain some lost momentum, a call comes in from his boss.

"Tommy! How ya doin'? Did ya see the game?" the manager wants to know. The chit chat continues, with Tommy impatient to get off the phone and back to work. But he knows that when his manager wants to talk, Tommy should listen because sometimes his manager buries a request, albeit not always urgent, in the middle of his chatter. So Tommy listens, staring at the documents on his desk, and murmuring polite "uh-huhs" until his manager hangs up.

Tommy returns to his AOC project and once again tries to regain his momentum. Everything's back on track, or so it seems. However, because he has lost his concentration by trying to sneak in some call-backs, he has barely gotten started with his AOC task. By now, Tommy's optimism has begun to diminish. So he says to himself, *"Please, please, boss, no more interruptions."*

"Please, boss, **no more interruptions!"**

9:10 a.m.
Back again on his AOC project, a staff member walks in to remind Tommy that he is still waiting to receive Tommy's coaching before meeting with a new client. The coaching session takes 20 minutes.

9:30 a.m
Once again Tommy returns to the AOC task, making serious headway. But in the back of his mind is the knowledge that during the previous hour he had ignored several incoming phone calls and emails that he feels obliged to address. He sets aside the AOC task to return the calls and emails. In the course of doing so, he makes promises to clients and colleagues, so he quickly fulfills them, again pushing off his AOC task.

11:40 a.m
Tommy endeavors to integrate the callbacks into his workload. Added to his frustration about not getting his AOC task done is his fear that his inability to concentrate all morning will cause him to make some error. He puts out a few unexpected fires while the clock keeps ticking and his anxiety about his unfinished AOC project keeps rising.

12:20 p.m
Tommy is now undeniably and uncontrollably frustrated. Looking back he feels that, although he's been working very hard trying to complete this two-hour AOC project, he has barely made a dent. Worse, now that he's late for lunch, his energy is flagging and he feels a little light-headed. Nevertheless, he postpones lunch until 1:00, but eats at his desk because he has a client meeting scheduled at 1:30. For the first time that day, fortune smiles on him; the client calls to cancel.

Looking back he feels that, although he's been working very hard trying to complete this two-hour AOC project, **he has barely made a dent.**

45

Clients and colleagues who interrupt Tommy notice his uncharacteristically grim face and the edge in his voice. His stress is accumulating. Tommy has now entered the **Helter-Skelter Fibrillation Zone:** the zone of distress.

1:30 p.m

Tommy's gratitude for the cancelled lunch soon evaporates. Beginning at about 1:30, client calls come in non-stop. Though stressed to the max and depleted of energy, Tommy feels obliged to take these calls – these are clients and colleagues, after all. So he takes them, and hopes that he handles them well given his state of mind.

3:40 p.m

Tommy returns to his AOC project, grimly determined to complete it no matter what. He reviews what he got done before, only to be startled to discover that because of all the interruptions, he made some serious calculation errors. He has to start over! Now that marvelous good mood and optimistic outlook of the morning is entirely gone. Clients and colleagues who interact with him notice his uncharacteristically grim face and the edge in his voice. His stress is accumulating.

Tommy has now entered the Helter-Skelter Fibrillation Zone: the zone of distress.

4:00 p.m

At this inopportune moment, his manager calls with a reminder that his AOC report is due by 5:00. Tommy starts to explain about the interruptions that derailed him and is shocked to hear his manager's response: *"Tommy,"* he says. *"Your problem is that you don't know how to manage your time. Why do you allow yourself to be interrupted?"*

The weight of this question hangs in the air.

"And," he adds. *"Don't leave without finishing that report."*

Tommy now feels humiliation on top of his distress. He feels he has been working hard all day to accomplish what he vowed to do at 8:30. How has this come to pass?

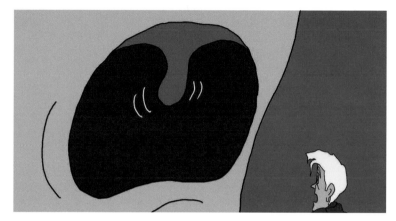

4:30 p.m

The next thing he knows the day is almost over, but his AOC task remains incomplete. He has disappointed his boss and must now disappoint his wife and his clients because he is having an AIAI attack. That's right, as the renowned cardiologist Dr. Meyer Friedman said, the combination of Aggravation, Irritation, Anger, Impatience has plagued him in waves all day and will send Tommy to the AIAI Hospital. (Unless of course if he is from New York like me, in which case AIAI is in our DNA.)

Tommy now feels humiliation on top of his distress. He feels he has been working hard all day to accomplish what he vowed to do at 8:30.

If there were such a thing as an AIAI electrocardiogram, Tommy's Monday would look like this:

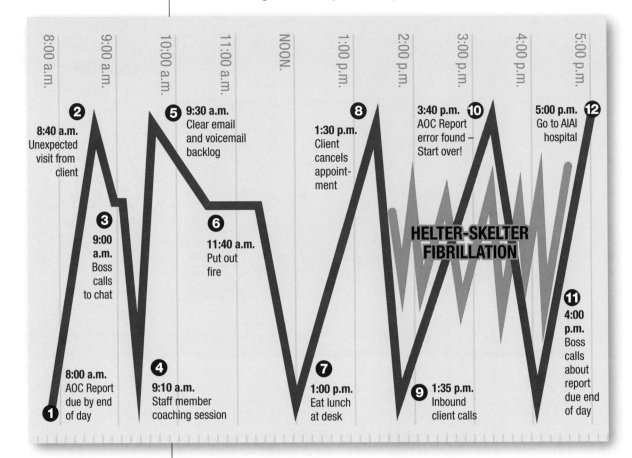

8:00 a.m.
9:00 a.m.
10:00 a.m.
11:00 a.m.
NOON.
1:00 p.m.
2:00 p.m.
3:00 p.m.
4:00 p.m.
5:00 p.m.

❷ 8:40 a.m. Unexpected visit from client

❺ 9:30 a.m. Clear email and voicemail backlog

❽ 1:30 p.m. Client cancels appointment

❿ 3:40 p.m. AOC Report error found – Start over!

⓬ 5:00 p.m. Go to AIAI hospital

❸ 9:00 a.m. Boss calls to chat

❻ 11:40 a.m. Put out fire

HELTER-SKELTER FIBRILLATION

❶ 8:00 a.m. AOC Report due by end of day

❹ 9:10 a.m. Staff member coaching session

❼ 1:00 p.m. Eat lunch at desk

❾ 1:35 p.m. Inbound client calls

⓫ 4:00 p.m. Boss calls about report due end of day

Of course, Tommy is fictional, but is he a total exaggeration? Do you not have days – too many days – that find you grim and unhappy as the day winds down, frustrated by interruptions that kept you from your most important duties and spoiled your pleasure in good work well done? Take a moment to walk yourself through your own typical day and week. How many unwanted interruptions can you count up? How did you do in our Interruptions Quiz?

From my experience training executives to maximize productivity, quality control, and client sales and service results, Tommy isn't an exaggerated scenario at all. They tell me that days like his lead to their feeling unproductive and incompetent, which leads to a loss of self-confidence, self-esteem, and job satisfaction. Their colleagues and clients notice it. The progressive build-up of stress from interruptions leads to palpable *distress.*

Yes, the usual term is stress, but I use the word *dis*tress advisedly. First, stress is a fact of life – we couldn't avoid it if we wanted to. And it's not always negative, as in death, taxes, divorce, anger, etc.

There are also the positive benefits and thrill of **eu-stress. Eu-stress** is what people feel at some of their most positive moments – getting married, winning the lottery, and so on. Athletes use eu-stress almost like fuel to compete and win.

What Tommy needed was help in managing his stress so that it didn't turn into distress. Distress (or what I like to call stress run amok) made him feel confused, dysfunctional, fatigued, and unproductive. Think about that the next time you are overcome by those feelings. You don't have to eliminate stress from your workday; you just need to learn how to keep it from morphing into distress.

Race cars have tachometers so that drivers know how far to push the engine. Tachometers register the engine's revolutions on a green-to-red continuum. In the red zone, the engine is over-revving, running too fast for the gear. This over-taxes the engine and can cause it to wear out faster or even burn out. But in the green zone, speed matched to gear, shifting at the right juncture, the engine runs fast, smooth, and long, without undue wear and tear.

In the red zone, the engine is over-revving, running too fast for the gear. This over-taxes the engine and can **cause it to wear out faster or even burn out.**

Symptoms

Diagnosis

Treatment

So can you, if you can keep your normal workday stress from turning into distress.

A medical doctor would be sued for malpractice if he prescribed treatment without understanding the cause of his patient's symptoms, so let's invoke the **Medical Model** here: symptoms, diagnosis, treatment.

This **Medical Model metaphor** helps us better understand that before any of us can seek or recommend a treatment plan to overcome what ails us, we must first, like medical doctors, diagnose the cause and the effect of the symptoms.

The Medical Model metaphor helps us better understand that before any of us can seek or recommend a treatment plan to overcome what ails us, we must first, like medical doctors, diagnose the cause and the effect of the symptoms. In distress management, as in medicine, proposing a treatment plan before first diagnosing the cause and effect would be malpractice.

Many workplaces are guilty of time management malpractice and thus ignore the destructive effects of what could otherwise be easily resolvable causes.

It's these causes that we're going to concentrate on from this point forward wherein the effect of "overreaching productivity goals and objectives" in the workplace may be resolved simply by eliminating the 5 Time-Loss Factors.

What I'm going to share with you is why and how these factors impact us physically, psychologically, emotionally, and, ultimately, functionally as well.

Researchers have pointed out the fact that in many instances the effects of the distress caused by the inability to manage time (as a result of the 5 Time-Loss Factors) ranked as high as unemployment, divorce, and even death.

As I began to flesh out the cause and the related psychological and physiological effects, I couldn't help thinking about David Letterman's late night show. So, ladies and gentlemen, allow me to present *"The Time Bandit Solution Psychological, Emotional, and Spiritual Top 10 Effects Caused by Interruption-Driven Distress." (See graphic at right.)*

TOP 10

EFFECTS CAUSED BY INTERUPTION-DRIVEN DISTRESS

 10 **Misunderstood** by my Time Bandits because of their inability to correlate interruptions with time management needs vs. excuses; they probably think I'm lazy, incompetent or rude.

 9 **Unappreciated** because they don't understand that I'm working as hard as I can to get all that needs to be completed as fast as I can without making mistakes.

 8 **Confused** because I don't know how to explain or get the Time Bandits to cooperate by helping me eliminate the cause and effects of the 5 Time-Loss Factors.

 7 **Insecure** because of the impact of the 5 Time-Loss Factors on my productivity results vs. their expectations.

 6 **Frustrated** because I'm misunderstood, unappreciated, confused, and insecure.

 5 **Low Self-Esteem** because of my feeling that someone other than me could do a better job explaining to Time Bandits how and why I need their help.

 4 **Rejected** because when I try to explain and ask for any form of respite from interruptions, I am ignored or turned down.

 3 **Mental and Physical Exhaustion** because of the energy-zapping impact I experience during my battle against the 5 Time-Loss Factors.

2 **De-motivated** because I feel that the Time Bandits don't care one way or the other about the 5 Time-Loss Factors and/or anything else that affects my productivity and/or my job satisfaction needs.

And now, ladies and gentlemen, as David Letterman used to say, "and the #1 effect caused by the 5 Time-Loss Factors is...."

1 ## Hopelessness
because I've given up thinking that it's within my power and/or capability to resolve the causes and effects of interruptions.

It wasn't Tommy's busy day that caused distress. The given reality for Tommy and most of us "Tommys" is that every day has a boss, customers, deadlines, and duties. One of the main reasons that sent our Tommy off the rails was all his interruptions – interruptions that he didn't know how to handle.

To bring home to you just how psychologically deleterious the Time Bandits and the related 5 Time-Loss Factors are, I developed an interruptions-related distress management matrix for the purposes of revealing and differentiating the causes of distress versus the psychological effects of distress.

CAUSES VS. EFFECTS MATRIX

AIAI   (AGGRAVATION, IRRITATION, ANGER, AND IMPATIENCE)

EFFECTS

1. Hopelessness
2. De-motivated
3. Mental/physical exhaustion
4. Rejected
5. Low self-esteem
6. Frustrated
7. Insecure
8. Confused
9. Unappreciated
10. Misunderstood

The object of the matrix is to increase your understanding **of how the various causes of distress** correlate with effects.

CAUSES

The object of the matrix is to increase your understanding of how the various causes of distress correlate with effects. We will start the process with another one of our self-assessment exercises to identify the causes of distress you may feel. First think about what time-related events happen that leave you feeling distressed. List those causes on the matrix in the space provided. Then, review the list of effects, and check off the effects that correlate to each distress cause.

Any of these effects can send your emotional tachometer right into the red zone. As we know from our basic experience with the red zone, it's a place where you simply don't want to stay for any length of time because it's one of the most unproductive places to be on the planet.

What's YOUR distress type?

We don't all experience distress the same way and for the same reasons. This was brilliantly demonstrated decades ago in research conducted again by Dr. Meyer Friedman, in his popular book, "Type A Behavior and Your Heart."

According to Dr. Friedman, Personality Types A and B may suffer from the same causes and effects of time-management pressure, but at markedly different levels and with markedly different reactions. From my own research about time management, I have determined that there is a Type C personality as well.

You are probably most familiar with his **Type A Personality,** generally perceived as highly productive, aggressive and intense which, in turn, can at times subject them to an increased risk for early heart attacks. In a nutshell, as it pertains to time management, Dr. Friedman's Type As believe that there is simply never, never enough time in a day, week, month, or lifetime to do all that needs to get done within given deadlines. As a consequence, they stay revved up to the red zone. They get a lot done, but to the untrained observer they may rarely appear happy and relaxed.

In my own experience with those Type As in my life, I find that they not only get a lot done, they also seem to maintain a sharper focus and greater tenacity, which in turn helps them get more out of life in terms of business opportunities and friendships. For this, one can't help but admire them.

You are probably most familiar with Dr. Friedman's **Type A Personality,** generally perceived as highly aggressive and at an increased risk for early heart attacks.

To be happy and stress-free, **Type Cs must feel that they are extremely organized** so that they can achieve total quality control in all they do.

His Type B personalities will look at the same reality – the same tasks, the same deadlines, the same times, and appear to be confident there's always plenty of time. As a result of this perception, they often take on more than they can do and then struggle with their deadlines as well. Regardless, they usually get as much done as Type As, skip the heart attacks, and seem to lead longer and apparently happier lives.

My Type Cs are perfectionists, satisfied with nothing less than absolute perfection – hence never satisfied. We see this in Type C students for whom getting the top grade on a test is not enough if they did not get every answer right in every detail. Anything less than perfection is failure. To be happy and stress-free, Type Cs must feel that they are extremely organized so that they can achieve total quality control in all they do. To feel completely organized, however, they always need more time. Like Meyer Friedman's Type As, Type Cs never have enough time.

The Type Cs in my life excite my admiration for different reasons from Type As. They are orderly and organized, cautious and deliberate. When perfection matters, I want Type Cs on the team. Your pilot, your surgeon – you don't want them to be comfortable with the occasional failure.

So, to recap. Type As seem to live in almost constant distress that there's not enough time to get their stuff done. Type Cs live in almost constant distress that there's not enough time to achieve perfection. Time is an enemy of the As and Cs, while for Type Bs, time is a friend – there's always plenty of time.

As Doctor Friedman and I contend, if humanity consists largely of these three types, it's no surprise that we have wars. It's just amazing that we ever find a way to work together. Imagine how we torment one another. I can tell you exactly how. I am a Type B, so I am blessed with all the time in the world: in fact, *"What else can I take on to fill all this lovely vacant time that stretches before me?"*

For those of you, like me, who are Type Bs and do not directly suffer from the causes and effects of Type A or C behavioral symptoms, when working with them you may be suffering indirectly in the same way that we non-smokers suffer from second-hand smoke. I call this panic transference.

Here's a personal example of what I mean.

Pity my Chief Financial Officer and colleague, Ruben, a Type A. I am his nightmare. We generally work together "separately," but occasionally circumstances have us collaborating hand in hand toward a hard deadline.

I see deadlines the way Columbus taught us to see the horizon: not edge-of-the-world cliffs that we'll tumble over to our perdition, but brush strokes on the scenery that will remain way out there where they belong, no matter how close we sail. The only thing that makes me desperate about a looming deadline is the idea that I must turn away things that come up in the meantime. *Of course we will get it all done.*

Not so Ruben, equally loathe to say no but with a different view of time. To him "deadline" is two words. You flirt with missing one under pain of death, and it's a line, not an evanescence. If time is "what keeps everything from happening at once," I am its undoing and his. While his entire history is one of meticulously meeting deadlines, there is never a moment when he is confident that there is enough time to do so.

My blitheness only exacerbates his worry. His discomfort infects me. When I experienced Ruben's discomfort, like a chameleon, I found myself morphing from Type B to Type A, becoming impatient and short with my staff as a deadline loomed. Thrown together under the nearing deadline, we each find ourselves dedicating as much energy to calming the desperate child within us as we do to the work itself.

Type As live in almost constant distress that there's not enough time to get their stuff done. **Type Cs** live in almost constant distress that there's not enough time to achieve perfection. Time is an enemy of the As and Cs, while for **Type Bs,** time is a friend – there's always plenty of time.

You realized that 30 days is infinite, so you did other things. Until about Day 29, when **you realized barely any work had been completed.** Panic set in and the rest is painfully familiar.

Or pity my wife, the perfect Type C, a Harvard graduate with a Masters in Structural Engineering. Her closets and desk are as neat as pins (thimbles and sewing needles arranged by size!). Books on shelves, all arranged by category and alphabetized within each category. Files completely organized and immaculate.

When she undertakes a task, she starts at the background level, researching everything that could possibly have a bearing. Through it all, she will say that she never, ever has enough time to achieve perfection. Do you think she finds it helpful when I assure her that it's wonderful when a tiny flaw is visible to her?
And spare some pity for me. After all, we Type Bs are not without our own time-related distress – the panic of the confirmed procrastinator. Of course we procrastinate – it would be insane not to. If there's always enough time, then why wouldn't we use "now" for other matters that come up?

If you're a Type B, then you remember your school days, when you had an essay to complete and the teacher gave you 30 days to complete the task? You said to yourself, *"Easy. I will just work on it every day for an hour and by the time the month is over, it will be a piece of cake."* So what really happened? You realized that 30 days is infinite, so you did other things. Until about Day 29, when you realized barely any work had been completed. Panic set in and the rest is painfully familiar.

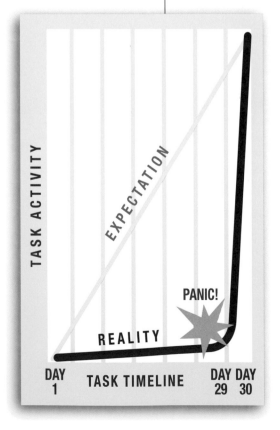

So we Type Bs *do* recognize what As and Cs feel most of the time – we just save it for the last minute.

Whether you are more like my CFO, my wife, or myself, be assured that, like the three of us, when you've completed this book, not only will you learn techniques for dealing with your time-management distress, but you will also learn how to cope with your own personality type and those of the people around you. You will feel fully protected by your own customized time-managed step-by-step implementation action plan.

For now start thinking about your personality type when it comes to time and workflow management. Take a deep dive into a better understanding of who you are, and like Ruben, my wife, and me, how you react to time management pressure.

Think honestly about whether you feel you can never get enough done because no matter how hard you work there's never enough time. Or do you feel that no matter how many tasks you complete, if there's no perfection, and I mean complete perfection in what you do, the completion is unsatisfactory? You don't just need an A, you need an A+. Or are you one of the extraordinary few who see yourself as traveling on a sea of time in which, because time is flexible, you can fit everything you need to do into it? Or do you see a combination of these personality types, perhaps influenced by those close to you?

Now that you've determined your personality type, I now want you to analyze how your personality type reacts and/or overreacts to ordinary time management issues.

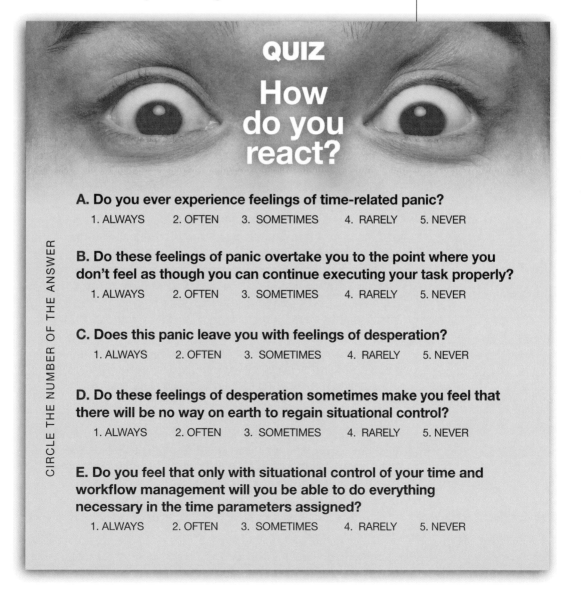

QUIZ
How do you react?

CIRCLE THE NUMBER OF THE ANSWER

A. Do you ever experience feelings of time-related panic?

1. ALWAYS   2. OFTEN   3. SOMETIMES   4. RARELY   5. NEVER

B. Do these feelings of panic overtake you to the point where you don't feel as though you can continue executing your task properly?

1. ALWAYS   2. OFTEN   3. SOMETIMES   4. RARELY   5. NEVER

C. Does this panic leave you with feelings of desperation?

1. ALWAYS   2. OFTEN   3. SOMETIMES   4. RARELY   5. NEVER

D. Do these feelings of desperation sometimes make you feel that there will be no way on earth to regain situational control?

1. ALWAYS   2. OFTEN   3. SOMETIMES   4. RARELY   5. NEVER

E. Do you feel that only with situational control of your time and workflow management will you be able to do everything necessary in the time parameters assigned?

1. ALWAYS   2. OFTEN   3. SOMETIMES   4. RARELY   5. NEVER

For you to outrace the number one cause of all time-related distress, unwanted and unnecessary interruptions, is of great importance.

If the sum of your answers is less than 20, I urge you to read the following chapters in great detail. For you to outrace the number one cause of all time-related distress, unwanted and unnecessary interruptions, is of great importance. You see, by doing so, you will also eliminate all the Type A, B, and C panic and the painful backfire effects of the 5 Time-Loss Factors.

But also remember that however you have handled interruptions, and the resulting distress in the past, you've been doing it for a long time, and your habits have hardened. And if you've had success, take care in noting that you might be attributing that success to those habits when, in fact, your success might have come *despite* those habits. If I spent time looking backward, I might well wonder how much energy I invested in heroically entertaining interruptions instead of wisely deterring them.

So what I'm asking of you as you read, in addition to everything that you're about to learn, is that you remain patient and stay focused as we delve into the solutions portion of the book to help you deal with the number one cause of time management distress, interruptions, as told from my own personal history.

Time Loss Interruption Solutions

In the Time Loss Interruptions Solutions section, you will learn how to gain control over those unwanted interruptions by gracefully training and negotiating with the Time Bandits who unwittingly steal your time.

"The Child is the Father of the Man."

— WILLIAM WORDSWORTH
(FROM "THE RAINBOW")

Quiet Time

Do you ever feel as though life is out of control? Like you're riding a very fast merry-go-round and can't get off? When you have an important decision to make, do you feel pressed to decide it even though you haven't had sufficient time to give it proper consideration?

And even if you appear to be successful and in control, are you afraid you'll be found out as just being lucky … or an imposter?

Remember: *"If you don't control your time, you don't control your life."* You may be suffering from what I experienced in my early life – a toxic combination of fear of failure AND fear of success. I was helpless to overcome the stressful effects of those fears until I learned about "Quiet Time." Teaching you about Quiet Time is my gift to you now.

I was five years old when it happened. In an accident, I lost my right eye.

There, I wrote that. Here I am 70 years later – happy, beloved, respected, busy, and successful – yet writing that simple sentence was excruciating. I wrote this entire book knowing that sentence needed to be written, but that I could only write it after the rest of the book was finished.

Bear with me here – my revelation is for you as well as me: I'm going to tell you why it took me so long to understand the damage interruptions do and to cherish what I call Quiet Time, and I hope my story eases your own journey to the same destination.

Ed Brown, his sister Rhoda and mother Rachel on the day of the accident in 1941.

What Teddy Roosevelt's daughter said of him *("He wants to be the bride at every wedding, the corpse at every funeral, and the baby at every christening.")* was not far off from me in my desperation to deny or obliterate my handicap.

Just seeing that first sentence above can still make me dizzy with the grief and pain of the original experience. It can make me flush with the embarrassment and anger I felt when anyone noticed my handicap or teased me – or when I thought they did.

Those feelings don't linger because I rationally think my loss was the worst thing that could ever happen to anybody. Of course I know of worse tragedies, and so do you. But it was the worst thing that ever happened to that little five-year-old. We only have our own story to live, to rejoice in, to suffer from, to learn from.

My loss created a new me. I doubt my life would have unfolded as it did if that accident had never happened. In my child's mind, my loss had to be compensated, and I had to do the compensating. Success would be my revenge. *"Nothing succeeds like success."* I went over the top. I had to be the most popular kid in any group, the best athlete at every sport, the winner of every contest and every argument.

What Teddy Roosevelt's daughter said of him *("He wants to be the bride at every wedding, the corpse at every funeral, and the baby at every christening.")* was not far off from me in my desperation to deny or obliterate my handicap, my defect, my unwelcome different-ness.

Did I succeed? Of course not. How could I be the best tennis player when half the time I couldn't see the ball? How could I be the best basketball player when I was several inches shorter than most of the starters? Nobody is popular with everybody. Nobody wins at everything. True, my raging zeal and determination made me achieve more than most would ever have expected of me, but even when I did excel at something, there was still the glaring reality: my eye was still gone.

I look back at old photographs and see now what others saw then: an even-featured, well-formed young man, glowing with youth and lightly marked with a forgettable flaw, no more disconcerting than someone else's freckle-splashed forehead, gap-toothed smile, or bald pate. But by then my *modus operandi* was over-achieving and over-compensating. The world owed me for my loss, and I was going to extract that debt payment every day in every way.

This was sub-conscious of course; I never spoke of my accident or acknowledged my impediment to myself. Classmates, teammates, teachers, and coaches knew better than to mention it, and so did my family. But at age 19, when I moved from New York to Los Angeles, determined to make it in the music industry, about all I brought with me was the chip on my shoulder, my burning zeal to show the world, and my secret vow: *"Before I hit*

30, partially sighted or totally blind, I will be a successful man."

I kept the vow. Early on, I finagled meetings with all the right people – the right artists, musicians, managers, producers, and so on, turning their talents to my benefit and theirs. There came a day when I had a huge fish on the line. I was in a bidding war for The Johnson Brothers, two songwriters who I knew could make me and themselves a fortune. My competitor was an established music industry genius, **HB Barnum,** who besides having an extraordinary eye for talent could play every instrument in the orchestra.

Secretly impressed, I forgot all about the Johnson Brothers and fell in love with HB, and we are partners to this day (and currently co-producing a rock opera).

If I'd been half as reflective then as I was ambitious, I might have slowed up to wonder why HB, a genius established in the business, picked a raw, striving kid from the East Bronx to be his partner, but my busy new life left no time for reflection.

I was only 22 years old when our record, "Tan Shoes and Pink Shoelaces," became the Broadcast Music Incorporated (BMI) "Record of the Year." It rose to number one in Cashbox and Billboard and stayed there for six months. It made top ten in the charts of every major country.

I was only 22 years old when our record, "Tan Shoes and Pink Shoelaces," became the Broadcast Music Incorporated (BMI) "Record of the Year."

Pink Shoelaces

Dodie Stevens

Citation of Achievement
1959
presented by
BROADCAST MUSIC, INC.
to
PIONEER PUBLISHING COMPANY
in recognition of the great national popularity attained by
PINK SHOELACES

I relished the accolades, prestige, and money, and with each heady success I would believe for a moment, an hour, or a day that I had finally been compensated for my cruel loss. But shortly the old feelings would return.

The royalties flowed our way. So did every major label and almost every major R&B group asking for our help: Aretha Franklin, Lou Rawls, The 5th Dimension, Little Richard, and Frank Sinatra. HB and I could do no wrong. I was the confidante of celebrities, adviser to the stars. I had a label, three publishing firms, and a business management firm.

So, finally, was I content and relaxed? Not in the slightest. Of course I relished the accolades, prestige, and money, and with each heady success I would believe for a moment, an hour, or a day that I had finally been compensated for my cruel loss. But shortly the old feelings would return. Outwardly I celebrated; inwardly my old grievance meter was running on high, insistently warning that my success could vanish in the blink of my one good eye.

And always, always over-compensating was how I conquered. So I dove into more and more businesses, reaping success hand over fist in one business after another.

Many of my clients, which included doctors, TV and motion picture actors, producers and directors, along with a whole host of live entertainers and athletes, needed tax shelters. Because tax rates in those days were up in the 90% range, I diversified into heavy equipment leasing and time sales finance lending.

In order to fill a desperate need, in the late '50s and '60s, I became an expert in capitalizing on tax loopholes and, in the process of learning how to do so, I went to work for a lawyer who managed superstar clients such as Doris Day, Kirk Douglas, and Burt Lancaster.

My reputation as a first-rate negotiator and investment manager flourished. This new business became so popular it generated scores of additional business management clients.

TOP: Kimo McVay; Bill Forman, owner and general manager of Cinerama; Don Ho; and Ed Brown.

ABOVE: Ed and actress Dorothy Lamour.

RIGHT: Roy Rogers

ABOVE: Horseback-riding with TV star Lee Majors, singer Don Ho and Ed Brown in the 1960s.

By then I already knew Roy Rogers, King of the Cowboys, who was business-managed by the wonderful Jim Osborne, then getting on in years. (As I will explain later, I also become Roy's partner.)

Jim and I liked and needed each other, so we formed the Osborne Brown Agency, eventually becoming, in billings, the third largest of its kind in the country. And our clients were happy to invest where the banks had been leery!

Then along came a famous magazine publisher who evidently saw more in me than I recognized in myself. I was astonished when he quickly partnered with me in several businesses. And then he further shocked me when he asked me to personally manage the film and television careers of 300 of his models.

> Then along came **a famous magazine publisher** who evidently saw more in me than I recognized in myself.

So there I was in my 30s, living a fantasy life. I owned a diversified conglomeration of businesses, I had a huge circle of great friends, I ran with an amazing crowd, and it was more fun than this Bronx boy had ever dreamed existed.

Surely now I was a happy man? Oh, I liked the bragging rights, and the optics were as gratifying as anything a young man could dream of, but as the saying goes, *"Be careful what you wish for."* There are two paths to unhappiness – not getting what you want, and getting exactly what you want, especially with **no time** to enjoy it.

In reality I was distressed beyond measure. My life was basically an explosion of interruptions. I had no peace. Everybody wanted a piece of me every day and every night, and thought they were entitled to it – and who was I to say they were not? Their careers and/or fortunes were in my hands.

Although he rarely would, if Roy Rogers wanted to call me early in the morning and say, *"Ed, I'm in the 91% tax bracket and I'm 62 years old (or, as he put it, '26 turned around'). I'm tired of paying for them to build ships for the Korean War and not having anything left for my estate planning. I need your help,"* who was I to be too busy to listen to him even if I couldn't always solve his problem?

Or if one of the models called me at 3:00 in the morning to say, *"Mr. Brown, I was told that if I posed in his magazine you would make me a star. What are you doing about it?"* She deserved an answer, and her fair shot at stardom.

It was not unusual for Pat Boone to drop by and say, *"I wanted to let you know, Ed, that while you were out of town I decided to purchase the San Francisco Warriors basketball team and I need your opinion about whether or not this was a wise decision."*

And as a fiduciary, everything I did, every decision I made, whether I had time to think it through or not – and increasingly I did not – could have grave legal consequences. I mean, I adhered to the highest ethics, but I was totally self-taught—diligent but un-credentialed, with all the insecurities that go along with a lack of credentials.

I was now negotiating

employment contracts with Warner Brothers, Columbia, and Capitol Records. Under my direction, my clients were making or not making huge investments and signing career-altering contracts that required my careful, thoughtful, massively-time-consuming consideration, talent, and knowledge. Yet, pressed for time – feeling like a hurricane inside a tornado – how could I not be making some impulsive decisions?

There was, however, another effect of this frantic, aggressive, bring-it-on way of doing business. If you never take a few quiet moments to ponder decisions, let alone a few quiet moments to think about their results, or, God forbid, take some pleasure in good results, you just feel like you're tightrope-walking at full speed. You reach the safety platform and go, *"Whew, made it one more time – I wonder how."* And then you're off again. You never build confidence in your own gifts.

You aren't even sure you *have* any god-given talent except maybe luck.

When I would read a press account of what a great negotiator I was, I'd think, *"Fooled him. Haven't been found out yet."* That's a depleting way to live – all activity and no reflection.

Besides, I don't care how much chutzpah you're blessed (or burdened?) with; at some point common sense raises its cautionary hand. Perennially short of time, I knew I was making knee-jerk, Hail-Mary decisions…then lying awake worrying about them. I had become Tommy Wants-to-Please! I even developed a stress-related heart condition.

I had no peace. Everybody wanted a piece of me every day and every night, and thought they were entitled to it – and who was I to say they were not? Their careers and/or fortunes were in my hands.

So in my 30s, I simply said to my LA life, *"Enough – no mas!"* I dissolved all my partnerships, sold off my assets, said goodbye to my clients – movie stars, athletes, singers, and all. I moved to Hawaii, intending to retire.

As soon as the plane took off, I felt my head begin to clear. Once settled in Hawaii, relishing my peaceful, quiet solitude, I could draw on my training in hatha yoga and transcendental meditation. I could perfect techniques I had acquired for meditative relaxation.

In Hawaii **I embraced my need for Quiet Time** as a poet embraces a muse.

Out of this solitude an epiphany emerged. For the first time since my five-year-old self had decided the world must pay me back for my devastating loss, I began to feel more than just compensated. I began to see life through a different lens. All my early, material success notwithstanding, I realized that it was this "Quiet Time" that I found more fulfilling.

Away from the LA carnival and chaos, I could think. It was easy to recall the times when I had been most productive in my pell-mell entrepreneurial life. It was when the press of too much pressure, noise, worry, or work forced me to withdraw just enough to let my mind work without interruption.

But I had never truly appreciated this Quiet Time or realized it was like oxygen to my thinking life. In fact, sometimes my retreat into Quiet Time had almost seemed like a weakness.

No more. In Hawaii I embraced my need for Quiet Time as a poet embraces a muse. I told my five-year-old self, *"You and I, we did just fine. We took our pain and loss, turned it into a driving force, made our mark, and did good for a lot of people. Now it's time for a new focus. From now on, let's you and I measure success not just with money, prestige, and influence, but also with the peace and joy of Quiet Time."*

Finally, that five-year-old was "relieved of duty," having, as Wordsworth said, fathered the man who now rose to the occasion. I could put all that overcompensating behind me and enjoy its fruits as sweet, not bitter.

So that was my new vow, and I steadfastly endeavored to resist pleas from LA to return to my old business. Sandy beaches, sea breezes, sunsets – it was a peaceful easy feeling.

But this tranquil life was about to explode with new opportunities for more show business fun and challenges than LA had held for me, because I was to meet the incredible, wild and unpredictable man who would change my life's course, Don Ho.

Don was then just a locally known entertainer. It took me about five minutes to hate the guy. His shtick was to demand that newcomers join him on stage and *"Tell a joke, sing a song, or buy the house a round."* Still painfully self-conscious, I did my best to get in the spirit of things:

Don Ho: *Hi bra'. What's your name and what do you do?*

Me: *I'm Ed Brown, a business manager.*

Don: *A what? What that mean? A business what?*

Me: *I'm a business manager; I help my clients make business and financial decisions.*

Don: *You're a booo-keepah!*

Thin-skinned, I bristled, but tried to put on a good face. I tried to tell a joke, but it fell flat. Don promptly ordered me off his stage: *"Hey bra', you bettah stick to your booo-keeping!"* It was a lousy start to what was to become a great friendship and partnership.

But this tranquil life was about to explode with new opportunities for more show business fun and challenges than LA had held for me, because I was to meet the incredible, wild and unpredictable man who would change my life's course, **Don Ho.**

Don Ho became an international star, and the pair of us went on to have more fun than any two guys could have prayed for.

Because even in my hot embarrassment, as I watched and listened to Don, the gears had started turning. If you have a passion and talent for something, you don't just switch it off. Watch any old flyboy look longingly when a plane thunders overhead. Or watch a long-retired investor overhearing young guns discussing a new business venture prick up his ears. I may have been seeking Hawaiian Quiet Time, but the business and personal management experience accumulated in me saw the potential in Don Ho.

In short order, Don went from that seedy little bar in a rough part of Honolulu to become the greatest and most profitable Hawaiian entertainer who ever lived.

Together, Don and I created his remarkable music career, and opened restaurants and nightclubs together. He sang and I produced his huge hit, "Tiny Bubbles," and then I landed, created, and co-executive produced "Hawaii-Ho" which was, at that time, one of the most expensive and most highly rated variety TV specials ever produced.

Don became an international star, and the pair of us went on to have more fun than any two guys could have prayed for.

You can see where all this was going, even if I couldn't then. I was being consumed again by the same thing that had sent me into "retirement" in Hawaii. I had changed states, but I hadn't changed my habits. Here I was, living what I knew most of the world would consider a charmed life, but I was once again without my oxygen – my **Quiet Time.**

But there was more to it this time. I was beginning to feel that I was meant for something more than the entertainment industry. By now I had realized that I was more than lucky – I was evidently pretty good at a few things, and wouldn't it be great if I could teach others what I had learned? I wanted my Quiet Time back, but I also wanted something different than another show business success – something that challenged me more intellectually and also served other people somehow.

I had learned the hard way: you don't manage celebrities *and* have a life of your own. I had once again sacrificed Quiet Time – which I knew was precious to me and hard to come by – because of where my talents and inclinations led me.

Looking back, I don't want to be too hard on myself for this mistake, but I learned an important thing from it. First, I realized that changing our embedded behavior is one of the hardest things we all do, even when we recognize that we must. I won't say we are all "hard-wired" to take a certain path, but I think we are "soft-wired" and it takes a lot of effort and discipline to alter ourselves to any visible extent.

So I made my way back to Los Angeles, determined to regain Quiet Time composure and confident that I would figure out the next chapter of my life. The pain of the five-year-old was slowly but surely yielding to true understanding.

I was about to learn how desperately the corporate world needed to learn the same lesson.

As I explained earlier, it wasn't until after I initially completed writing *The Time Bandit Solution* that I then elected to add this additional Quiet Time chapter. I did so with the hope and belief that I could transfer to you all that I learned about the benefits of Quiet Time (and the pain of its absence) so that it could add quality and value to your lives as it eventually did mine.

Quiet Time serves to protect some of our rarest and most important resources: clarity, enlightenment, and peace of mind. Your life successes may very well depend on your ability to somehow manifest Quiet Time so that you can reap the benefit derived from decision making during focused concentration. That's not to say that Quiet Time guarantees better decisions – you still have to do the work – but it creates an environment where good decisions can flourish.

How many times have you asked yourself the proverbial question, *"Oh, what to do, what to do?"* Only to find yourself in reflection, because of indecision or inaction, years later, saying *"I coulda' I shoulda' I woulda'"* or *"If only I had known then what I know now."* Why does this occur? Because every behavioral change in life, including the quest for Quiet Time, is loaded with comfort-level and *"I'm just too damn busy"* time management-related challenges.

> Quiet Time serves to protect some of our rarest and most important resources: **clarity, enlightenment, and peace of mind.**

Quiet Time is not something conjured up like a Marvel comic strip superhero yelling *"Quiet Time!"* instead of *"Shazam!"*

Whether it's in the everyday workflow or the flow of your personal life, changing our behavior requires us to make the hard decision of leaving that comfort zone and overcoming the fear of the unknown. In my case, my decision was leaving show business but that may not be the way it is in your life.

Certainly we will all eventually come to forks in the road of life as though they were gauntlets, and we will choose to either pick them up or not. If we make the wrong decision, we face what may very often be deleterious, unintended consequences.

Be clear. I'm not suggesting that you seek Quiet Time to become rejuvenated, inspired, or more motivated about your career, marriage, or golf handicap; quite the opposite. I'm suggesting you find Quiet Time only to make those very important decisions.

It as simple as this: within a high-quality Quiet Time environment, the odds are you will make high-quality decisions. Conversely, in a low-quality Quiet Time environment driven by chaos and pathos, it's more likely that you'll make low-quality decisions (i.e., mistakes) or decide to just procrastinate or, as people like to say about Congress, *"kick the can down the road."*

I've been told by others that my whole concept about Quiet Time being an achievable skill is an idealized "blue sky" dream. But they are mistaken. It *is* an achievable skill, not something conjured up like a Marvel comic strip superhero yelling *"Quiet Time!"* instead of *"Shazam!"* So am I saying decision making and utilizing Quiet Time is a process, not just an intuitive knee-jerk reaction for problem disposition? You bet!

I became so dedicated to the concept I ended up referring to it as the **Quiet Time Upside/Downside Process.**

The Quiet Time Upside/Downside Process has the following Big 5 steps for learning how to know when Quiet Time, as a solution for resolving confusion and for important decision-making purposes, is not just an option but a critical must.

Step 1

Understand what is it you are trying to decide that requires an Upside/Downside Process Quiet Time-enabled focus?

● What is the immediate upside benefit?
● What is the immediate downside risk?

Similarly to every investment analysis (i.e., return on Investment (ROI), return on effort (ROE)), life-altering decisions all have risk/reward ratios. Understanding this concept is the essence of the Upside/Downside Process.

Step 2

Understand what is it about the decision that confuses or challenges you?

Step 3

Analyze, once the decision is made, how do you actualize/operationalize that decision in such a way that discomfort, let alone risk, is mitigated?
Do you create a contingency plan (Plan B)?

Step 4

Decide by when must that decision be made?
By when will the effects of that decision be concluded?
Remember that decision-making action plans, without deadlines, are akin to procrastination.

Step 5

Decide how much of that decision has to be made immediately? How much can be deferred?

The Quiet Time
Upside/Downside Process

The Process is how I conduct my self-interrogation and apply these 5 steps involved in a particular decision I must make. As I said in Step 1, the analysis begins by asking yourself whether the risk you're taking and the downside potential loss is worth the discomfort you may feel from leaving your comfort zone and accepting a dramatic behavior change, capital investment, even health risk?

You can also mentally place your decision making on a **Risk/Cost Matrix** where the X axis is the *risk* of being wrong about a decision, and the Y axis is the *cost* of being wrong.

For example, if I'm picking out a silk scarf to bring my wife Shari after a long trip to Asia, the risk is very, very high that I will get it "wrong" – that had she been there with me she would have chosen a different design. However, the cost of that wrong decision is virtually zero. She will be glad I remembered her and will forgive her husband's questionable taste as every happily married woman does.

If, on the other hand, I'm about to be videotaped teaching a new module of one of our successful behavioral change solutions, the cost of my doing it wrong would be very high – disappointed customers, lost revenue, diminished confidence of my employees. But the risk of my botching it is probably low because I've worked very hard for many years to do it especially well.

In neither case would I treat my decision or preparation lightly, but neither would I need to create a Quiet Time hiatus before I bought the scarf or decided how to deliver the videotape lecture.

You can mentally place your decision making on a **Risk/Cost Matrix** where the X axis is the risk of being wrong about a decision, and the Y axis is the cost of being wrong.

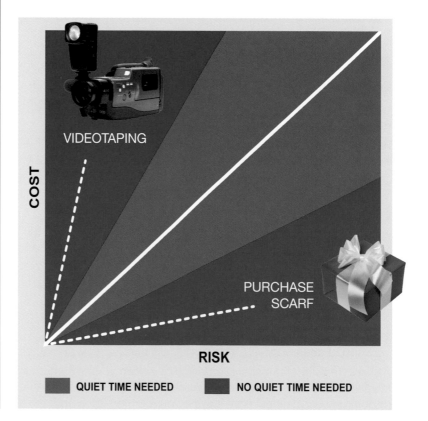

VIDEOTAPING

COST

PURCHASE SCARF

RISK

QUIET TIME NEEDED   NO QUIET TIME NEEDED

But in my life and yours, there are many moments when, with the aid of the Upside/Downside Process, we realize that this is a complex and life-decision-making challenge.

By example, do you hire or fire? There are few things in your working life that are more momentous than that – you have power over someone else's career, possibly their family's happiness, their financial well-being – to say nothing of the best interests of your company. Both the risk and the costs are very high so, in the matrix, the closer my risk/reward ratio is to the solid white line, the greater the need for a Quiet Time hiatus.

But here's the tricky thing. You don't always see your Quiet Time needs coming. Sure, you know in the morning that you're going to hire somebody that day, so you can plan to Quiet-Time your decision. (Yes, I use it as a verb.) But you take calls all day long without knowing what urgent matters are coming from the other end that may also need Quiet Time.

Consider your own version of calls like these:

- *"We had to close the line because our supplier ran out of materials, but if we switch material suppliers, we may put him out of business."*
- *"I just heard that our best salesman is about to get a different job offer."*
- *"User Acceptance Testing just called, and they want to meet with us all weekend long."*

Obviously, the first thing you need is more information, but then you are going to be called upon to make a momentous decision. Are these other issues urgent enough to require Quiet Time?

Beware of mistaking urgency for clarity! That's what I felt back in the days when I was making way too many financial decisions for way too many demanding celebrities. They made me feel matters were urgent when, in fact, what was needed was contemplation.

If people are sitting there staring at you expectantly and waiting for your decision so they can get their work done, that's a pretty powerful impetus for announcing a decision and looking decisive. We tend to think we will be admired if we act decisively. We worry we will look tentative or even weak if we say, *"Thank you, give me some time to think about this, and I'll get back to you with my decision."*

But here's a good thing to remember for such moments: uninformed decisiveness is dangerous; deliberateness, as long as it isn't paralyzing, is an underrated virtue. There's a sweet spot, so you need to cultivate your urgency/clarity communication

We worry we will look tentative or even weak if we say, *"Thank you, give me some time to think about this, and I'll get back to you with my decision."*

If we humans were less complicated, in fact **if we were nothing more than automatons,** the complexities and the conflicts surrounding decision making might be a matter of data analysis, number crunching, statistics, and forecasting.

antennae. You need to coach your Wants-to-Please self to listen to your Wants-to-Ponder self. Both are important team members!

There are, of course, situations that are completely obvious candidates for Quiet Time. Life decisions; do I marry this person? Stay in this marriage? Do I take this job? Should I resign? Do we let the kid back in the house if he relapses? Do we start this charitable organization?

If we humans were less complicated, in fact if we were nothing more than automatons, the complexities and the conflicts surrounding decision making might be a matter of data analysis, number crunching, statistics, and forecasting. However, human nature keeps us leaning towards our natural inclinations versus simply weighing the data.

For that reason, I developed the following **Quiet Time Quiz** designed to help you better understand whether or not you would be better off with the benefits of Quiet Time.

So, please, do what I did and ask yourself the following questions:

Quiet Time Quiz

Are there decisions, dreams, and concepts that you have suppressed or sublimated because of your fear of unintended consequences?

1. Always   **2.** Often   **3.** Rarely   **4.** Never

Have you made changes in your life forced by events over which you had no control?

1. Always   **2.** Often   **3.** Rarely   **4.** Never

Do you wish, when you had to make a decision, that you had been able to have Quiet Time?

1. Always   **2.** Often   **3.** Rarely   **4.** Never

If you were able to find Quiet Time in your life, would it be helpful in terms of important career or life, health and happiness (not just wealth-related) decisions?

1. Always   **2.** Often   **3.** Rarely   **4.** Never

Do you know the consequences of just using intuition versus Quiet-Timing carefully thought-through decision making?

1. Always   **2.** Often   **3.** Rarely   **4.** Never

If, by adding up the total of all your answers to the quiz, the sum is 10 or less, then you, like me, are in need of Quiet Time.

Time Locking
has changed
the lives of
many for the
better – and
can do the
same for you.

In the next chapter, I will describe how I took my
life-changing revelation about Quiet Time and, through an
onion-like progression of revelations, turned it into a
formalized set of practices that we called **Time Locking**,
which has changed the lives of many for the better – and
can do the same for you.

All men's miseries derive from not being able to sit in a quiet room alone.

— BLAISE PASCAL

Time Locking

Quiet Time usually means time spent alone, and frankly I have always felt that "alone" could use better PR. Greta Garbo made being alone sound intriguing. Gilbert and Sullivan made it melodic. Many poets made it rhyme.

But usually "alone" is a loser. I know a lot of people and you probably do, too, who dread sitting in a quiet room alone. Maybe they have experienced loneliness and conflated it with solitude. Maybe they worry they will appear friendless. Or maybe they are simply habituated to the distraction of others. Like city people spending the night in the country, they are unnerved by the quiet.

The world at large often agrees on the unbecomingness of alone. Go unaccompanied to most fine restaurants and notice the pity on your behalf. Book a travel tour and pay an astonishing premium for the presumption of not sharing your room.

"He was a loner," neighbors always say of the suddenly infamous miscreant next door. *"Single by choice – just not mine,"* says the rueful divorcée in a popular movie.

Okay, got it. Alone sounds like a loser.

And yet, is it? After all, how many painters lay on their backs on the Sistine Chapel scaffold? How many pilots settled into the cockpit of the Spirit of St. Louis?

There is **a universal need for quiet, alone, uninterrupted time** whether you are in the corporate, academic, or non-profit world – or retired, or a student, or a busy stay-at-home parent.

How many agonized presidents scribbled those notes on the train to Gettysburg? How many poets withdrew to Walden Pond? The Muse never visits during staff meetings or conference calls. She waits until she will be noticed, indulged, and rewarded.

Clearly, great things, otherwise unattainable, emerge from working alone, quietly, uninterrupted.

And let's be clear that "alone" doesn't have to mean a sole individual. Workers today increasingly work in teams. Virtual, protean, floating, or permanent – teams are an essential way of getting work done. The virtues of working "alone" apply to those teams, too. When they can close off the rest of the world, focus single-mindedly on a unified goal, protected from interruptions, that's when these teams are, for all practical purposes, working "alone" like the great people mentioned above.

This is easier for some teams than for others, obviously. The more homogeneous the members of the team, the easier they will find it to focus single-mindedly on a goal. Regardless, there is clearly a universal need for quiet, alone, uninterrupted time whether you are in the corporate, academic, or non-profit world – or retired, or a student, or a busy stay-at-home parent.

Or for that matter a burnt-out manager of celebrities.

I had allowed my life to become a cacophony, not once but twice. My five-year-old's idea of "making it" or "showing the world" was to be popular and admired. In Hollywood, that morphed into wanting to be talked about, sought after, and lauded – constantly. In Hawaii, that morphed into a creating a world-wide sensation and hanging out with the boldest of the bold-face names. Seductive, but unsatisfying, and never, never any solitude.

Now, back in LA, fully appreciating the value of Quiet Time, I was invigorated. I didn't know where life would lead me next, but by now, having found I could make a great living at almost anything I touched, at least I wasn't worried, and surely I would not remake old mistakes I had already learned from. I vowed that this time I would keep a firm grip on Quiet Time, but not by becoming a hermit, lone traveler, or retreating to some mountaintop. I knew I enjoyed people and business and problems. I knew I was good at learning something from almost every encounter, and using those lessons to solve business problems.

It was time to find a business that would capitalize on my experience but *also* my needs as I now understood them. I said to myself, *"Do this, Ed, so long as it does not put you back into the maelstrom of confusion that deprived you of all that wonderful Quiet Time you found."* Could I have one without the other?

But if I wasn't going to take responsibility for whole lives and careers any more, what was there in my history that was valuable and not overly intrusive? I found the answer through a buddy who was doing sales for a popular motivational speaker, Robert Proctor. The company was not doing all that well, but I thought, *"Hmmm, instead of managing stars in the entertainment business, perish the thought, what about managing a more business-oriented personality?"*

So I joined Robert and learned the motivational business. Robert was amazing – he would hold his audiences in the palm of his hand as he would shout to the rafters in his 3.5-octave speaking voice, *"Courage conquers fear."* His audiences became so motivated you could practically watch them

It was time to find a business that would capitalize on my experience but *also* my needs as I now understood them.

It turned out that **motivation alone wears itself out** unless it's accompanied by serious behavioral change and a deep understanding of what to do and how to do it.

floating through the transom of the auditorium, but there was a flaw to the sustainability of his business. I remember watching him, awestruck, while he revved up a roomful of insurance salesmen to a fever pitch. But later when we followed up with the insurance company, it turned out that motivation alone wears itself out unless it's accompanied by serious behavioral change and a deep understanding of what to do and how to do it.

No problem – I began searching for how to take what I had learned from Robert but make it sustainable and valuable for businesses; taking it to the next level, if you will. That led to the formation of The Cohen Brown Management Group, where my partner Marty was front office – teaching sales and sales management, and I was back office – managing the firm and its finances, negotiating contracts, and scheduling Marty's appearances. I was happy in my role, and, I thought, reasonably well-fulfilled in my working ambitions.

Life rocked along sweetly as our reputation grew. Then suddenly we found ourselves in that perverse crisis that confronts every successful consulting company: we had more great business than we had senior consultants to deliver it. We had closed a massive piece of business with Merrill Lynch to assist them in decentralizing their entire, highly computerized operations, breaking it down into regions. But we were overbooked; unless I led the project, we would have to turn down the biggest most prestigious piece of business we could have imagined.

Courage or not, I knew that I had little knowledge of brokerage or white-shoe Wall Street. I was frankly terrified of doing it. But ultimately I was convinced by colleagues and Merrill's EVP that I could learn what I needed to know. The client knew of my success in the entertainment world, and knew me to be a self-taught man whose main talent was not celebrity management, but business problem solving of virtually any kind. He himself was not Operations "born and bred." In fact, he was considered a Johnny-come-lately to Operations, so he had a point to prove himself by demonstrating his confidence in a somewhat unorthodox choice like me. His confidence was, by itself, inspiring. And when I predicted that solving Merrill's computer decentralization was going to be about 10% technology and 90% behavioral change, it was settled, he wanted me.

And as you know by now, I handled intimidation by striding up to it and punching it in the nose. Being intimidated was pure motivation for that one-eyed, five-year-old scamp – the same person, now slightly older, who used to demand to bat clean-up in baseball, play center in basketball, and carry line one in tennis.

We were overbooked; unless I led the project, we would have to turn down the biggest most prestigious piece of business we could have imagined.

While I was frankly having heartburn at the size and visibility of the Merrill project, the little boy inside of me was saying, *"Ed, this sounds impossible – let's you and I do it!"*

I read, I went, I killed. Or, in the more genteel parlance of Merrill Lynch, I found a solution. The solution...a combination of my experience using Quiet Time and all of what I had learned from Robert and Marty regarding human behavior and its psychological components.

I read,
I went,
I killed.
Or, in the
more genteel
parlance of
Merrill Lynch,
**I found
a solution.**

Merrill Lynch's operations

were in tight quarters on Wall Street. They planned to move to larger quarters, but the move had been delayed. My assignment was to investigate what I was told was a problem with the night shift of the 24-hour data processing department. The night shift wasn't meeting their deadlines, even though it was staffed, equipped, and managed comparably to the day shift that preceded it.

I went to the center one night already fairly confident of my working assumption: I was going to see some obvious workflow problems and maybe some poorly trained people. So imagine my surprise when I arrived to find a smooth-running operation – a calm, quiet, speedy, efficient beehive of workers, heads down, working hard. I'd been in plenty of ops centers before, and this was as peaceful and harmonious an operations environment as I had ever encountered. I was glad I had kept my working assumption to myself!

Next, I visited the day shift. In total contrast to the tranquility of the prior night, I thought I'd entered an arcade. It was over-crowded and chaotic. Overlapping conversations created a din. Phones rang and rang, and voices escalated to be heard over other voices. Desks crammed the hallways, and people couldn't avoid barging into each others' spaces or bumping into others' desks. It looked like bumper cars at a local carnival, not collaboration.

After making these observations, and then asking the supervisors a few questions, the problem quickly became clear. In this crowded, chaotic environment, the day personnel simply couldn't get their work done, so they were either late transitioning over to the night shift, or leaving unfinished work for the night workers to figure out. As I discussed earlier in the Causes versus Effects Matrix, the night personnel efforts to solve the problem mistakenly looked like the cause of the problem. The cause in this case was actually day processing's chaotic environment.

That was the short answer and we proceeded to solve the problem. But the bigger revelation for me was the incredibly destructive power of interruptions. Of course a crowded environment isn't as good as an un-crowded one, but there was more going on than space problems.

What fascinated me was that the day shift people were just as dedicated, skilled, and hardworking as their night shift colleagues. But while an almost inviolate environment let the night workers function uninterrupted, the day workers were subject to endless interruptions – whether from a phone ringing, or being bumped while they worked, or overhearing a nearby conversation. All these interruptions drained away their concentration and energy, upending their productivity because of the 5 Time-Loss Factors.

What was my immediate thought? To quote Yogi Berra, *"it was déjà vu all over again."* Me, managing 300 models, receiving phone calls at all hours of the night, and making massive financial decisions with little time to reflect. Call it vicarious, empathetic, or

Desks crammed the hallways, and people couldn't avoid barging into each others' space or bumping into others' desks. **It looked like bumper cars at a local carnival,** not collaboration.

Just like me, they too needed Quiet Time, but they couldn't pick up and go to Hawaii – **they had to keep coming into this chaos** every morning and sticking with it until evening.

idiosyncratic, but *I knew how these people felt and I knew what they needed to survive.*

Just like me, they too needed Quiet Time, but they couldn't pick up and go to Hawaii – they had to keep coming into this chaos every morning and sticking with it until evening. I knew we could fix the problem if we could come up with a workplace version of my Hawaii interlude. Not a one-off event but a true change in their workflow and methodology. If Quiet Time was strategic, I needed something tactical; a cultural shift, a new work paradigm – from an interruption culture that was only exaggerated by their overcrowding.

Then I thought of something my partner had said when I'd asked him how he managed to excel at so many disparate pursuits: public speaking, corporate consulting, and counseling individual patients.

"Ed," he told me. *"Unlike you, I do one thing at a time. Obviously, if I'm on stage giving a speech, I don't take calls from patients.*

*Well, the reverse is just as important: when I have a patient in my office, there is no such thing as a phone call or any other interruption, not even the so-called urgent call from the CEO of my biggest client. I may not lock the door, but I definitely **lock my time**."*

So the solution for Merrill Lynch, where they had no doors to lock, had to deal with locking their time against interruptions. And because it had to work for all of these people if it was going to work for any of them, it had to become a formal methodology, with rules, accountability, and real learning and behavioral change – a process.

We recognized that we had an almost laboratory-like opportunity to delve deeply into the workplace bane of interruptions. We could conduct a real-world comparative analysis of the productivity of the two groups – night and day processing.

We were able to extend our research when the data processing department was finally able to move to new quarters. There, in a proper working environment, we took my "Quiet Time" experiences and began to create an early version of what ultimately became **Time Locking.**

So what exactly is Time Locking?

To Time Lock is to voluntarily commit yourself (and to get a commitment from your Time Bandits) to become empowered and enabled by them such that you may work within pre-determined blocks of uninterrupted time.

To enable them to organizationally Time Lock, I developed a series of step-by-step minimum daily action Time Locking rules. *(See next page.)*

So the solution for Merrill Lynch, where they had no doors to lock, had to deal with **locking their time against interruptions.**

Rule 1

Each person had to Time Lock for at least one hour per day, during which period the Time Lock was strictly enforced and quality control assessments were conducted by members of the quality control division. No one was permitted to invade those Time Locks, not even upper management.

Rule 2

Even supervisors would limit their interactions with subordinates only to as-needed interactions, and never, never during the Time Locks.

Rule 3

All administration, operations, and compliance personnel would receive Time Locking training, so that all team members would understand the purpose of Time Locking, respect its boundaries, and have the opportunity to participate in their own Time Locks.

Rule 4

Individuals would be bonused for increased productivity attributed to Time Locking.

Rule 5

Staff personnel were to cover for each other during each other's Time Locks.

After training them, we compared day processing's productivity to that of night processing, and roundly confirmed our hypothesis again. Having uninterrupted Time Locks made day processing's quality control productivity equal to that of night processing.

For this reason, we were not surprised to learn that eventually the productivity results of day processing grew so dramatically that they not only met their deadlines, but night processing generated time and workflow surplus.

With this time surplus they were able to set achievable higher standards and increased goals and objectives for operations day and night processing.

What we also discovered, however, is that Time Locking will not work without genuinely committed mutual agreements between the interrupters (Time Bandits) and the interrupted. This means, for Time Locking to become a solution for overcoming interruptions, both the Time Bandits and their victims must be of one mind, which is that Time Locking is in their mutual best interests.

When I teach this concept in a classroom setting, it's here that eyes roll, feet twitch, and the look of bewilderment and surprise is everywhere.

This is when they realize that the "price" of achieving the benefits of Time Locking is persuading their impervious, inflexible, inconsiderate Time Bandits to WANT to leave them alone – to change their behavior.

What?! Change somebody else's behavior?! I can almost hear you saying, *"Hey, Ed, you must be dreaming. It might work somewhere else, but not in this environment. Around here, interruptions are like a freight train traveling at warp speed, and you want me to stand on the tracks?"*

Wait. Wait. I promise you, this is entirely doable. I have taught thousands of executives how to do it, and not one of them got run over by a freight train.

If you keep turning these pages and trusting that I can do for you what I've done for thousands of participants in my classes, you will be holding all the cards when it's time for you to propose a Time Locking win-win regimen. You will, as Mark Twain is supposed to have put it, have *"the calm confidence of a Christian holding four aces."* By win-win I mean not just a win for you but a win for your customers, colleagues, managers, corporate stakeholders, and even your family and friends.

Ed Brown (left) receives an award for his work with Merrill Lynch.

I promise you, this is entirely doable. I have taught thousands of executives how to do it, and **not one of them got run over by a freight train.**

TIME LOCKING ℠
Please do not disturb

Our training, consulting, and problem-solving programs and solutions enhanced the Merrill Lynch retail and operations groups so dramatically that they became embedded within the culture of Merrill Lynch and, to my knowledge, may continue to operate to this very day.

I'm not suggesting you use **Time Locking signs** when it comes to your clients but you can certainly use them with your colleagues.

What we learned at Merrill Lynch wasn't just that a chaotic work environment is inimical to excellence or that a peaceful environment is healthier. We learned that people first need to realize the value of Quiet Time, so that they can overcome the crippling obstacle Pascal described ("not being able to sit in a room alone"). Then they need instruction in how to attain Quiet Time, and, finally, how to use it wisely. We learned that we could teach people to make solitude not a misery but a source of accomplishment and the joy that accomplishment brings.

When we completed our assignments, in retrospect we realized that what we learned at Merrill Lynch was just as important to us as what we taught. So as a result, when we returned to our offices in LA and formalized our commitment to Time Locking, we adapted it to our own environment. Now, we and our teams put Time Locking signs on our doors when we need them.

We ask our assistants to tell others that we're Time Locked. We don't break anyone's Time Locks unless it's an absolute emergency, partly because we respect others' need for Time Locking, but also because we understand that our best interests will be much better served when they can focus on our needs deliberately, not when we happen to interrupt them.

Because of this mutual value, we added another important feature to Time Locks: the Mutual Time Lock Agreement. By negotiating with your colleagues and your counterparts mutually acceptable Time Locks, you and they will be spared many interruptions, and you will also be spared the difficulty or inconvenience that someone else's Time Lock might otherwise cause you. Now we understand what kind of work is eligible for Time Locking and what is not. We agree on which periods of time are convenient for Time Locks and which are not.

Not only do we spare ourselves unnecessary time and expense, but we work more harmoniously as well. Not to exaggerate: we don't pretend that we've eliminated the arbitrariness of an entrepreneurial company beholden to clients operating on their own schedules in dozens of time zones. But we do carve out and protect time for what matters. You can be sure our finance department doesn't get pestered when they Time Lock to run payroll. My CFO Ruben can call me any time he wants, but he doesn't when I'm in make-up in the studio with camera crews waiting. And even I, Mr. Type B with my perception of infinite time on the horizon, no matter how excited I am about a new idea, will respect the Time Lock of a consultant who is finalizing a new contract proposal.

But more to the point (regarding what I suspect is worrying you right now), we don't just respect the Time Locks of our rainmakers and founders. It works both ways. Say I'm about to issue a peremptory request to my assistant and I then recall that she is Time Locking to complete a document a client is waiting for. Infringing on her Time Lock will set us all back. And I know that because she knew exactly how to negotiate her Time Lock with me: by conveying how it would benefit me, too. (Again, that's what you, too, will learn how to do in subsequent chapters – how to gain the cooperation of your Time Bandits when you wish to Time Lock.)

I'm not suggesting you use Time Locking signs when it comes to your clients but you can certainly use them with your colleagues. Even if you don't use an actual Time Locking sign, it's a good attitude to have to reduce the interruptions. You can use the jargon, *"I'm Time Locking."* It doesn't have the sting of *"I'm busy,"* and yet it firmly tells your colleagues, assistants, or any of your other Time Bandits that what you're doing is best done now without interruption.

By negotiating with your colleagues mutually acceptable Time Locks, **you and they will be spared many interruptions** and the difficulty or inconvenience that someone else's Time Lock might otherwise cause you.

So that's Time Locking: being alone, utilizing Quiet Time, and uninterruptedly doing what you must do in a way that makes doing it more efficient, productive, and possibly even delightful versus burdensome.

So that's Time Locking: being alone, utilizing Quiet Time, and uninterruptedly doing what you must do in a way that makes doing it more efficient, productive, and possibly even delightful versus burdensome. When I find myself possessed of a new idea that is bursting to be articulated – a new program, a new company, a new paper – I can't wait to Time Lock. Time Locking can bring focus and even joy, or at least serenity, to what would otherwise have felt like pressure and drudgery.

And Time Locking is not just for the average office worker, but valuable in any role. Consider parents. Is there any person who could better profit from the ability to compartmentalize and do a million things just right than the parent of dependent children? Parents are the ultimate multi-taskers of critical tasks – getting the kids to school and other appointments, managing the household budget, meeting dozens of deadlines, and all while keeping a positive emotional tone in the home. They need to be able to create time when it seems like there is none, to build uninterrupted momentum no matter how persistent the potential interruptions, and to find time for the "critical" tasks (building character in their children) as well as the "minor" tasks (indulging in leisure with them).

Likewise for professionals, such as lawyers, accountants, and doctors, Time Locking is a desperately needed tool. After all, when professionals offer their expertise, they often do so in the currency of time – billing by the hour. For many, finding time to "have a life" outside of their profession is a significant challenge. Most need to be skilled multi-taskers – moving smoothly among at least three domains: the practice of their profession, its administrative/compliance activities, and client/patient relationships. Imagine a surgeon unable to Time Lock around bedside visits, taking his brusque surgery manners to his patient interactions. Or imagine the lawyer taking his "lawyerisms" to the jury home to the dinner table or his kids' soccer games. Compartmentalizing those activities is a version of Time Locking.

And what student wouldn't be a better student if Time Locking were taught early and well? The distress of cramming for an exam could be reduced. Young students – and I mean really young – could be taught a youthful version of Time Locking that would help them deter interruptions and get their homework done with ease, instead of being pelted with distractions. College students would be able to combine a social life, and even a job, with good grades.

Now that you understand what Time Locking is and how it can be used, and for the moment, making the very large assumption that your Time Bandits will totally go along with your Time Locking proposal, please consider and answer the following questions.

What student wouldn't be a better student if Time Locking were taught early and well?

Q: **Which of your daily or weekly tasks would you choose to complete during a Time Lock for maximum efficiency?** (Would you make your outbound calls? Answer your emails? Write employee reviews?)

Q: **How would Time Locking benefit you?** (Would it prevent interruptions, restarts, do-overs, momentum loss, and related distress?)

Q: **What obstacles in your workplace make it difficult to Time Lock?** (Lack of coverage? Lack of space? Lack of understanding?)

Q: **Now that you understand how Time Locking would benefit you, consider how Time Locking could benefit your...**

   A. Customers and Prospects (better service, faster responses, better information)

   B. Colleagues/Team Members (more observation, more coaching)

   C. Your Manager (more reliable, more work accomplished)

   D. Your Family Members or Friends

So if you are still worried about how Time Locking will work in your environment, as they say in stand-up comedy, *"wait for it..."* it's coming.

Now that you know that Time Locking has mutual win-win benefits, you will need to accept the following challenge: how do I find the right words to articulate that benefits are mutual and not just one-sided? In the next chapter, you will not only learn how to answer this, but many other questions associated with palatability, desirability, and therefore the mutual benefits of Time Locking.

Proposing Time Locking

I know if you're like most of our STWM participants, and despite the fact that in the last chapter you identified the benefits of Time Locking, you're probably thinking, as they did, *"Ed, it's one thing to gain Time Locking cooperation from colleagues. But let's get real, **clients** are a whole different ballgame. How in the world can you possibly say to a client, 'I can't talk to you right now, I'm in a Time Lock!'?"*

My answer to you is…don't do that! Your clients will leave, and I wouldn't blame them! This said, the question is, how do you explain to the client that he would benefit as a result of Time Locking? And if you knew the answer, would you know how to articulate those benefits in such a way that the client would embrace and, in fact, perceive you as innovative, resourceful, and ultimately desirous of providing superior service? Would it make a difference if the client perceived you as "proposing" rather than insisting upon the Time Lock concept for him to consider?

Did I say consider?
Did I say propose? Yes.
In other words, you're going to have to negotiate with your client. You will get your Time Bandits to **want** you to Time Lock. I know that sounds a little like Tom

How in the world can you possibly say to a client, *"I can't talk to you right now, I'm in a Time Lock!"?*

TIME LOCKING

PLEASE DO NOT DISTURB

95

Sawyer getting the other boys to pay him to paint his aunt's fence, but with a crucial difference. You aren't just manipulating to make your Time Lock *sound* valuable. You are making your Time Bandit **understand** how your Time Lock serves his or her needs.

But don't worry. These next four chapters teach you, step by step, how to prepare for the particular occasion so that your Time Bandits not only don't resent your Time Lock; on the contrary, they will come to understand that Time Locks are in their best interests.

I came to learn this lesson from my own investment advisor, **Steve Antebi,** to whom I was one of the worst Time Bandits.

Steve Antebi,
President,
Maple Capital
Management
LLC; formerly
Investment
Advisor,
Bear Stearns

During a very volatile period in the stock market, when the market would fluctuate wildly, I would call him during trading hours and ping him with questions about this equity or that – why is it moving, what's going on? Now listen to his assistant Susie handling my interruption:

"Mr. Brown, how nice to talk to you, sir. You know, Steve, as you might expect, is doing some very important market research and in particular the equities in your personal portfolio. Would you like me to disturb him right now or is there anything I can do to answer any questions you may have?

What if she had said, ***"I'm sorry, he's busy. I'll have him call you back later"?*** Not only would I have been offended by the brush-off, but my anxiety about my portfolio would have spiked even higher.

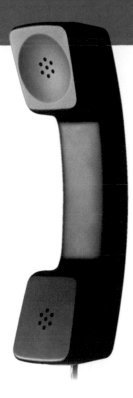

"Naturally, he told me that if you called and it was anything critical, I should definitely interrupt him. If it's not critical, then perhaps, Mr. Brown, I can set a phone appointment for you and Mr. Antebi for after market hours that would be mutually convenient?"

Here she was, firmly planted between anxious me and my broker, but do you think she irritated or offended me? On the contrary, I was impressed. Her professionalism and his made me realize I was in the hands of, well, professionals who let me know – in words and tone – that I mattered. And I was comforted: Steve was working on the very things I was anxious about. And I was convinced by her logic. Why in the world would I interrupt him if he's working on what I'm fretting about? *"Of course, thank you, let's set that appointment for after trading hours."*

A polite, professional, logical little speech – that's all it took to convert this Time Bandit – and to give Steve the Time Lock he desperately needed to manage my portfolio (and everybody else's as well).

They made it look easy.

But what if they had done it poorly?

What if she had said, *"I'm sorry, he's busy. I'll have him call you back later"?* Not only would I have been offended by the brush-off, but my anxiety about my portfolio would have spiked even higher. *"Later will be too late for what I'm worried about."*

What if she had put me through and Steve had said, *"Ed, I know you're worried but I can either talk to you or work on your portfolio, but I can't do both."* Factual, but rude – still making a customer feel inconvenient, not valued.

What if she had not explained what he was doing? It was her logic that made me realize I was on his radar, and he was taking care of my business. His Time Lock was my gain.

It was this "aha moment" in combination with my Merrill Lynch experience that was the quintessential, *summum bonum* challenge that once and for all motivated me to deliver STWM and write this book. After all, I had felt good about going along with Steve's Time Lock. It was just a matter of polite, direct, and clear communication in combination with a logical justification for the Time Lock.

In other words, because they were so smooth, I never even objected. By anticipating what I needed – politeness, comfort, assurance, logic – and delivering it, they overcame all the objections I would otherwise have voiced most strenuously.

After all, I had felt good about going along with Steve's Time Lock. It was just **a matter of polite, direct, and clear communication** in combination with a logical justification for the Time Lock.

That little speech of hers encapsulated a deeply embedded set of rules, discipline, and skill for overcoming potential objections of Time Bandits.

As would all of the other nervous clients who were, no doubt, calling Steve with the same worries and getting the same silken response from Susie.

But that silken response embodied a wealth of knowledge. Like the swan paddling furiously under water while gliding seemingly effortlessly across the pond, that little speech of hers encapsulated a deeply embedded set of rules, discipline, and skill for overcoming potential objections of Time Bandits.

They were so good that what they did requires four chapters!

- **In this chapter you'll learn** the "Rules" for negotiating within each of your Time Bandit Interruption Scenarios.

- **In Chapter 5:15,** you'll learn **how to anticipate and overcome any objections from your Time Bandits** – not only because you will likely get many objections but because your fear of them may inhibit your desire to negotiate Time Locking proposals.

- **In Chapter 5:30,** you will learn what it takes to be prepared to have the conversation and also how to prepare a personalized script for each of your Time Bandits. To assist you with your Time Locking Time Bandit proposal, you will receive Guideline Language with Key Elements and what I refer to as Time Lock proposal pre-scripting techniques.

- **Finally, in Chapter 5:45, you will learn** *how* to talk to your Time Bandits, bearing in mind that how you say it is as important as what you say.

The concepts and the Key Elements of the Guideline Language that I'll be providing come from 30+ years of real-world experience and each script can be easily customized for clients, managers, colleagues, family and friends.

Let's begin by going over the list of probable Time Bandits, and the rules for controlling them, starting with clients.

Reinforcing Time Locking against **client interruptions** might be your biggest challenge since the client is the lifeblood of any firm. Conveying the perception, for any reason, that you are under-servicing a client is counterintuitive to what you and your firm stand for. However, you will probably find that your clients are not offended if you know "what to say" and "how to say what to say" when training them, any more than I was when I was trained by my investment advisor and his assistant.

So what are the client Time Bandit rules?

Rule 1: **Client Call-in Interruption Scenario**

As Steve and Susie had done with me, educate your clients about how you run your business with respect to how to maximize client service. Since all clients know that you have a stockpile of clients, all of whom are entitled to the same quality of service, they'll fully understand and appreciate the fact that you cannot and should not be on the phone with two clients at precisely the same time. Thus, the most professional approach, Time Locking notwithstanding, is to make certain that you can provide the very best service to each of your clients by setting mutually convenient telephone appointments.

Time-managed appointment setting is particularly effective if the client requires more than just a few moments of your time to answer questions that require your research.

The best time to explain your Time Locking desires to your client is at the time you make your initial callback to the client whom you could not speak to because you were already on the phone with another client. Let your client know your Time Locking action plan, a script for which we will develop later and which will be of particular help if the client objects to setting a telephone appointment. You will be developing an excellent first-person response that your client will understand and accept.

Rule 2: **Client Walk-in Interruption Scenario**

You are speaking on the phone with one of your clients who cooperated with your Time Locking proposal (as per Rule #1) and another client comes by and sits at your desk, nervously tapping his foot waiting for you to get off the phone. Your mind is also on a report that is due within a half-hour to your boss and he is not the most understanding chap. So what do you do?

> The most professional approach to avoid client call-in interruptions is to **set mutually convenient telephone appointments.**

The same
rules that
apply to
**client
call-ins** also
apply to
walk-ins.

Well, the only difference between a walk-in and a call-in interruption scenario is that you'll be forced to allow the client who walks in on you to interrupt you at least one time. However, the same rules that apply to client call-ins also apply to walk-ins. By that I mean, after you politely respond to your client by satisfying whatever need precipitated their walk-in, before they leave, the timing will be perfect for you to educate your client about your Time Locking rules and gain their consensus.

If you were a walk-in client, would you be offended if, just before you left, I said to you the following:

*"Nancy, although I was **delighted** to see you and glad to have been of service, I **didn't expect you.** I have a lot more I'd like to go over with you. The reason I can't do it now is, unfortunately, **I have another client waiting**. What I like to do with my **best clients** is to set **phone or in-person appointments** during which I try **not to allow myself to be interrupted.** This ensures we have **quality time** where I can give you **my undivided attention** to attend to **your needs.** Let's pick a day and time that's **convenient for you** and **schedule an appointment.** However, should you ever have an **emergency**, please **don't hesitate** to call me at any time."*

Look, most of our clients are just like us. They're mostly considerate, well-mannered, and cooperative. Unfortunately, we'll always remember the ones that are not. Those clients might say, "Hey, I need you now and what's more, I don't care about your other clients. When I want you, I want you now."

Frankly, for all the years we have been teaching these skills no one has told us that they've ever heard this response before. So let's not overreact to extreme and unusual circumstances and throw away the baby with the bath water. However a good reply for this scenario could be:

"I understand. Let me tell one of my colleagues that I'm going to be working with you. Do you have an idea how much time we will need? That way, if any of my current appointments need to be rescheduled, I can let them know."

Naturally, if you have a lot of walk-ins, then you're going to have to make this same speech a number of times. What are your alternatives? As you'll find, over time these now-trained clients will have learned how you work, and why you work that way. In this connection, they will make appointments with you (or through your colleagues) or call you at a time you set aside for accepting calls.

Since these clients are cooperating with you, extend yourself by giving them the *very best service* that you can during your telephone or in-person appointment. Likewise, *thank them* for their understanding, patience, and for cooperating with your time-management needs. Also, let them know how accessible you are with respect to appointment setting.

My experience has been that when you set appointments with walk-ins or call-ins, your clients will have the same reaction I had when Steve Antebi's assistant so ably handled my interruption. Instead of complaining, they are likely to compliment you on the fact that you operate within a highly disciplined, professional structure and, in fact, will trust you more. Think how natural it is to make an appointment when visiting your doctor. So, why don't you get insulted about having to make an appointment? Is it because you acknowledge the fact that they are busy professionals?

We have been told by our clients that when they begin setting appointments like this, their friendship and bond with their clients actually grow, because their clients understand just how hard they work to be of service to them.

Next, what are the colleague and manager Time Bandit rules?

Over time these now-trained clients will have learned how you work, and why you work that way. In this connection, **they will make appointments with you** (or through your colleagues) or call you at a time you set aside for accepting calls.

Negotiating a **Mutual Time Lock Agreement** will be a simple matter of going over the benefits to each of you.

Rule 3: **Colleague Interruption Scenario**

You're a department head having a great day at work – making fast progress on your biggest project. At 10:00 a.m. you see an email from HR *"To all employees"* and you know, without glancing at the subject line, that they're announcing the new bonus program. You will your eyes away, refusing to open the email until you finish this project. You say to yourself *"focus, focus, focus."* But not two minutes later, another department head appears in your doorway. You know she wants to talk about implementing the bonus program in your group and so she says, as she always does, *"Got a minute?"* – Obviously expecting your usual answer: *"Sure, come on in."*

Since your colleagues, including your bosses and subordinates, probably face the same Time Locking challenges as you do, they, too, would very much like to gain situational control over their time by controlling their interruptions by training their respective Time Bandits as well.

For this reason, negotiating a Mutual Time Lock Agreement will be a simple matter of going over the benefits to each of you, to the point where they not only will agree to respect your Time Lock, but I believe they'll be enthusiastic, provided, of course, you respect theirs.

With the Mutual Time Lock Agreement, you have a great opportunity to negotiate an arrangement with your colleagues where they may cover your calls if you cover theirs, and provide some minimal task-related service to deal with walk-in and call-in traffic. Your assistants and colleagues can explain to your clients the fact that you are in a meeting and set phone appointments on your behalf. For your convenience, you'll find a sample Mutual Time Lock Agreement with Guideline Language in the **Appendix.**

Managers, more than anyone, will respect your Time Locks if they trust you and believe that respecting your Time Locks **will help you meet *their* deadlines.**

Rule 4: **Manager Interruption Scenario**

As with Tommy Wants-to-Please, your manager can be one of the most pervasive of all the Time Bandits, and if you are someone else's manager, you may be the most pervasive Time Bandit for your subordinates. Therefore, consider the fact that the same rule that applies to your colleagues could likewise apply to your manager. Hopefully, managers, more than anyone, will respect your Time Locks if they trust you and believe that respecting your Time Locks will help you meet *their* deadlines.

Here's a typical scenario. Your boss travels frequently to meet with customers. It's not unusual for him, on returning from a trip, to drop in on you unannounced and just "catch up" with you. It's always an interesting conversation – you like to hear what the customers are saying, and he often imparts essential information. But still, his visits are sudden, so you don't have an opportunity to rearrange anything else on your schedule. Also, the visits are lengthy, so you sometimes leave other employees hanging and often end up working late.

The script that I'm proposing you use is the same script that my colleagues use with me. They'll say:

*"Ed, I'm anxious to hear about your trip and equally anxious to meet your **critical deadlines.** However, to do a good job and meet the deadline, it will take my **full uninterrupted concentration,** and if it would be **acceptable to you,** I'd very much like to **set an appointment with you** later on in the day, or*

If your manager doesn't want to honor your Time Lock, then unless you're independently wealthy, I suggest you simply say, *"Of course, how can I help?"*

at another time after 3:00 p.m. In fact, what I **typically** do with my **other colleagues** that I'd love to be able **to do with you,** is to let them know in **advance** when I might have some **focused Time Lock needs.** So, Ed, **would you mind** terribly if I come to see you after my Time Lock opens?"

Another script that I like for managers and subordinates that my colleagues also use with me is this:

*"Ed, between 1:00 and 3:00 I'll be Time Locking to complete the **extremely important task you have given me.** I promise to **get back to you** at precisely 3:00 p.m. **Will that work for you?"***

You know, as their manager, it would be foolish of me to interfere with a subordinate's productivity. Unless, of course, what I need from them is more important.

However, I'm no fool, and neither are you. If your manager doesn't want to honor your Time Lock, then, unless you're independently wealthy, I suggest you simply say, ***"Of course, how can I help?"***

If, as they say, a journey of a thousand miles begins with the first step, these four rules are simply the first step. The second step, overcoming Time Bandit objections, will be covered in the next chapter.

Overcoming Objections

You might say we live in terrible times. Wars, poverty, illness, joblessness, homelessness are still with us.

But what about the case that we live in miraculous times? That we are so accustomed to advances that we forget to be amazed by them?

- We almost take for granted internet-based marvels that let individuals around the world engage in unprecedented intimacy, diplomacy, and understanding.

- According to the World Health Organization, *"Polio cases have decreased by over 99% since 1988, from an estimated 350,000 cases then, to 223 reported cases in 2012. The reduction is the result of the global effort to eradicate the disease."**

- The mortality rates of AIDS and cancer are lower than they have ever been.

- Education – the underpinning of hope for young people – is improving by leaps and bounds around the world.

- In the last 10 years, Africa's literacy rate has increased by 60% – after decades of failures.

These aren't just miracles. They are inspiration. To live in times like these is to be optimistic – hopeful and courageous. What a treasure of hope is in that cliché, *"If we can put a man on the moon, surely we can... (feel free to complete the sentence)."*

We have nothing to fear but fear itself.

— FRANKLIN DELANO ROOSEVELT, PRESIDENT OF THE UNITED STATES

* World Health Organization Poliomyelitis fact sheet www.who.int/mediacentre/factsheets/fs114/en/

We don't always fear the known – we fear the *un*known... Surely Michelangelo, Franklin, Lindbergh, FDR, or Thoreau heard more discouraging words than encouraging ones. Why didn't they fear failure enough to pull back and let somebody else brave the unknown?

You would think people who live in such times would be filled with confidence, self-esteem, and courage, wouldn't you?

But here's the difference. Those great things have already happened. They are knowns. We don't always fear the known – we fear the *un*known. You've watched a baby finally pull himself up by the edge of the coffee table – but then tremble to reach for the sofa. Even as adults, we seem fated to fear each unknown, no matter how incremental.

So after the joy of discovering Time Locking, you rejoiced that finally, finally, you could see a clear path toward eradicating the plague of interruptions that regularly destroy your productivity and peace of mind. But after a few minutes of rejoicing, if you're like most, I imagine you began to fear the new unknown: what your Time Bandit might say when you proposed your Time Lock:

- What if my client gives me an incredulous *"Do you know who I am?"* look when I propose making appointments? What do I do?

- What if my boss says, *"I'll set priorities around here,"* when I try to forestall his objection? How do I get out of trouble with him?

- What if my colleagues think I'm stuck up if I tell them I'm Time Locking? How do I assure them I'm not?

Surely Michelangelo, Franklin, Lindbergh, FDR, or Thoreau heard more discouraging words than encouraging ones. Why didn't they fear failure enough to pull back and let somebody else brave the unknown?

I would say they *did* fear failure, but they achieved greatness by knowing how to overcome their fears. For them, it might have been an innate skill. *If you could eradicate your Time Bandit's fear of the unknown, then miraculously would your own fear not also disappear?* If you were confident he or she would not object, then you would have no fear of rejection and could proceed with confidence. Imagine what great things you would attempt if you did not fear the outcome!

There are two ways to overcome fear of the unknown. One way is to face the "fear" as FDR suggested: throw yourself into the frightening place, somehow survive the terror, and (hopefully) come out fearless. High risk, uncertain outcome, and even if I were to recommend it, most sensible adults would refuse to take such an uncomfortable path.

Instead, I tackled the "unknown" side of the equation. Make the unknown less unknown. Become familiar with it in a small, low-risk way, so that when it's time to go all the way, fear has been replaced by confidence or at least a comfort level. In business, that's a pilot, or proof of concept.

Every inventor and/or business pioneer creates a road test, pilot or focus group built around the idea that a concept is only good or bad based on proof. They test. They take it in small increments. If you are a car maker, you run road tests, cracking up just a car or two while you figure out the right shape and placement of the bumper. If you are a television producer, you shoot just a few episodes and check the ratings before buying prime time and signing up stars long term. If you're buying software or training, you pick a small pilot group and compare results to a control group. Even if you're just selling gelato, you hand over a nibble on a miniature spoon.

That way, all parties can enter the transaction with a more carefree attitude of, *"What have we got to lose?"* If it doesn't work, we learn a lot. If it does work, we expand. We put the car into production, or the software across the enterprise, or the actors on contract. We buy the ice cream cone.

Every inventor and/or business pioneer creates **a road test, pilot or focus group** built around the idea that a concept is only good or bad based on proof. They test. They take it in small increments.

If you are a manager or part of a team, testing the efficacy of Time Locking could mean doing what we did at one of our large bank clients. Here were the instructions:

1. From a "functional point of view," select two identical departments or branches.

2. Make certain you establish a beginning baseline, and decide what behaviors and outcomes you want to track.

3. Within the first group, apply all the rules of Time Locking. Within the second group, it's business as usual—in other words, do nothing.

4. Run this pilot for 30–90 days.

5. Now measure the differences: above all, measure the amount of time saved by Group 1 vs. the time lost in Group 2.

Let the results speak for themselves.

At the conclusion of the pilot, we asked, *"Did your customer sales and service people find that Time Locking gave them more time to focus on direct customer interaction and sales, and if so how much more?"* The answer: 80%. Can you imagine how fast the control group branch managers demanded that their locations start Time Locking? I mean, when you consider that one of the biggest headaches for a branch manager is scarce staffing, imagine getting an 80% boost in well-trained staff! Now that's taking the unknown out of the equation!

But even if you are not part of an organization where you can control-group-test your Time Lock, you are not without "pilot" potential. You can say something temporizing along the lines of, *"Let's test whether my Time Lock really makes me hard to reach for you, or if in fact it makes me easier to reach."* Or, *"Consider permitting me to Time Lock three times and, if it's not working, then let's revisit the concept."*

Remember, by suggesting a time-limited commitment on his part, you are offering your Time Bandit a way to jettison his fear of the unknown so that your own fear of rejection evaporates. That's how you shift the thinking from fear-based objections to: *"Why not – I have nothing to lose!"* That's how I imagine our working-alone heroes handled it.

So we've left fear of the unknown at the side of the road, but objections are still in our path. Even after great pilots, people still have questions and objections, which is fine. You don't want your Time Bandit to respond to your Time Lock proposal with an indifferent, *"Sure, whatever."* If they do, they are saying they are indifferent or, even worse, they are not interested at all in what you are proposing!!

If you're like most of our STWM training participants, your Time Locking proposal will stimulate questions or objections. After all, you are proposing a significant change to people who probably think you're doing just fine now. You tap into their natural skepticism. To one degree or another, we are all inclined to greet new suggestions skeptically, or at least ask questions.

So remember this if you remember nothing else from this chapter: *Objections are not objectionable! The first "buy" sign of a prospect is sometimes an objection. That's right: Objections often = Closing. This fact has been proven in Cohen Brown's worldwide best practices regarding customer buying behavior, and it is core to what we teach about the Sales Cycle (i.e., Creating an Interest, Overcoming Objections, and Closing).*

In fact, as we like to say at Cohen Brown, *"Overcoming objections is the royal road to closing a sale."*

Oops, I broached it, didn't I? *"Sale."* When your Time Bandits object, you must persuade. What is persuading? It's selling.

Don't flinch at the word, because you sell all the time. You sell your spouse on where to have dinner, what to wear, what to

The first buy sign of a prospect is sometimes an objection. That's right: **Objections often = Closing** more often than not.

Don't flinch at the word "sell," because you sell all the time. **You sell your kids on picking up their toys, going to the zoo, and doing their homework.**

watch on TV. You sell your kids on picking up their toys, going to the zoo, doing their homework. You sold your boss on your project plan, your vacation days, and your resource needs. You sold your teammates on when to hold team meetings and what software to use.

If you're still flinching, is it because you are thinking of "selling" as crudely getting your own way over the preferences of others? But that's not what you did, is it? Hopefully, you didn't bully your spouse to end up at your favorite restaurant, or frighten the kids into doing the homework, or demand your teammates choose your software. Instead, I am sure you negotiated these things. You stated a preference, others stated theirs, you arrived at solutions that satisfied all (well, not counting the homework). You persuaded them by showing them the benefits.

That is, you used selling and negotiating skills. I've been teaching those skills to amateur and professional salespeople for decades. So when your Time Bandits ask, *"What's in it for me?"* or object, *"That sounds inconvenient,"* do not conclude that they don't want you to Time Lock. Conclude instead that they are interested, but… *But* they need more information. *But* they aren't clear about the value. *But* they would like to negotiate.

If your Time Bandits don't raise objections, then you don't know what persuasive tack is the right one. So, if you receive reasonable, benign objections, great – be grateful. Once you've heard their objections, you can be persuasive. You are traveling down that "royal road to closing."

Our clients consider the Cohen Brown Objections Clinics among the most beneficial programs we offer. They not only profit our clients, but they increase morale and self-motivation because our clients feel fortified by these techniques. I've actually heard some clients, following their Objections Clinic, evoke what we call the Clint Eastwood Principle: *"Go ahead, make my day. Give me your worst objection."*

As a sales consultant, one of the most important observations I've made about objections is that *not only* are objections not objectionable, they are also *predictable*. Why is predictable important? Because if you can predict an objection, you can write and rehearse your response.

Over the years, and as a result of running literally thousands of Objections Clinics, I appeared to become adept at memorizing scores of objections offered by my classroom program participants. I told them that I had the capacity to not only memorize hundreds of spontaneous objections, but also the ability to remember precisely what to say in response.

At first they thought I was just showing off, and tried to trip me up. They threw one objection after another at me. As soon as they came, I would say, *"Oh, these 10 objections are all the same, and they are all stating they have no need for your product/service."*

The next 10 objections would come at me, and I'd say, *"Those objections are also all the same, and they are explaining they fundamentally don't trust you or the benefits of the product or service."*

Just for the fun of it, I would imitate Johnny Carson's character Carnac the Magnificent pretending I had some magic sixth sense to be able to collate all of their objections. Eventually, I demonstrated to them, as I will to you, that all objections to Time Locking (and almost anything else in the way of a product sale or service) belong to one of these four categories:

1. No Need

2. Distrust

3. Inconvenience

4. I Don't Understand

You don't need to be **Carnac the Magnificent** once you learn that all objections to Time Locking fall into one of four categories.

Everything you ever do that involves other people will be easier and happier if you can quickly detect **if what you hear them say is an objection,** and, if so, what kind it is.

No Need

Distrust

Inconvenience

I Don't Understand

You need to commit these four to memory for the rest of your days. I'm serious. Everything you ever do that involves other people will be easier and happier if you can quickly detect if what you hear them say is an objection, and, if so, what kind it is.

Because let's face it, another common human trait is an inclination, when we feel put on the spot, to be evasive, indirect, or vague. We don't say what we mean! We're not malicious or duplicitous. We're just trying to get through life without giving or receiving any more friction, irritation, or pressure than absolutely necessary. So when people don't say what they mean, you had better be good at figuring out what lies underneath.

How did I arrive at just four objection categories out of so many possibilities? Let's go through an exercise. When you propose Time Locking, and you hear any of the following:

1. *"We're doing just fine."*
2. *"I have enough challenges without taking this on."*
3. *"Time Locking? I'm already too busy. Time Locking is just one more thing to do."*
4. *"We've always had an open door policy."*

Aren't these four objections all saying **"I don't need** what you're offering?"

And how about:

1. *"Why should I trust you?"*
2. *"How do I know that you won't be on Facebook during your Time Lock?"*
3. *"Who put you up to this?"*

Aren't these three objections, when you drill down, basically **Distrust** objections?

What are different ways of saying **Inconvenience?**

1. *"I don't have the time to implement Time Locking."*
2. *"I'm very sorry, but now is not a good time to discuss your proposal."*
3. *"I'm very late for an appointment."*
4. *"How long will this presentation take?"*

How about objections associated with **"I don't understand** what you've said?"

1. *"I'm very confused by your proposal."*
2. *"Am I committed or can I change my mind?"*
3. *"Exactly how does all this work?"*
4. *"How will you present Time Locking to your clients and colleagues?"*

These objections all sound different but when you boil them all down, there are just four.

Think of the four categories as a file cabinet containing all objections.

Let's start this process by writing down on a sheet of paper all of the objections you can think of or predict that you might hear from all of your Time Bandits when you explain Time Locking.

Think of the four categories as a **file cabinet** containing all objections.

For example:

1. **How will Time Locking work in our environment?**
2. **How will Time Locking affect our relationship?**
3. **How will Time Locking affect your relationship with others?**
4. **Why now?**
5. **How will Time Locking benefit me?**

_____

_____

_____

_____

Now look them over and see if you didn't write two or more objections that, although written differently, are actually the same. If so, collate those into one objection. Next, categorize the remaining objections into one or more of the four objections categories.

It is always your obligation to educate a Time Bandit about the benefits and features of any proposal.

To become your own "Clint Eastwood," you need to first predict relevant objections (as you just did), and now create **If/Then Scenarios,** *"If they say this, then I'll say that."*

Let's say you were trying to sell me something, and my objections were voiced as logical questions, such as: *"May I ask, what are the benefits of your proposal?"*

Would that question make you feel threatened? Or intimidated? Or in any way uncomfortable? Wouldn't you think, *"If I were in his shoes, I'd ask the same thing."* And wouldn't you suppose I was expressing interest?

It is always your obligation to educate a Time Bandit about the benefits and features of any proposal. Example: *"Mr. Time Bandit, I believe I found a way forward to dramatically increase my quality control productivity as well as dramatically increasing the quality of my service, etc."* followed by your description of Time Locking.

How would you feel if the objection you heard was: *"How do I know that what you're telling me is valid?"*

Would you be offended? Or would you be as honest with the Time Bandit as he/she had been with you when voicing the objection? And if you heard that objection, would you know how to respond? Or would the objection be so off-putting that you panicked and ran? Or by putting yourself in the Time Bandit's shoes, did you utilize accurate empathy?

The "No Need" objection, no matter how dogmatic it may sound, is a clue-based test question. The Time Bandit is basically saying, *"Unless you can convince me that I do have a need, I'm going to assert I have no need."* Imagine going to a doctor who tells you that you need surgery, would you not seek a second opinion? Yes, that is what we do. A patient is entitled to listen to a second opinion, as is the person who believes that he has no need for what you are proposing.

But how would you feel if you were contacting a brain surgeon in the middle of an operation, and he said, *"I have no time right now for your questions."* Would you take that personally?

You shouldn't.

This is just an "Inconvenience" objection and should be taken literally. All the prospect is stating is that they're willing to talk to you, but at another time.

How would you feel if you were contacting a brain surgeon in the middle of an operation, and he said, *"I have no time right now for your questions."* **Would you take that personally?**

And if after making your Time Locking proposal your Time Bandit said to you, *"I hear what you're saying but I really don't understand,"* would that stop you in your tracks? No, you would make it your responsibility to explain and educate further, wouldn't you?

Why does it matter that there are only four objection categories? Because for every category you must have a response. So instead of having to learn many of them, you only have to learn four – these four:

Category 1: **No Need ... Second Opinion**

Category 2: **Distrust ... Feel/Felt/Found**

Category 3: **Inconvenience ... When will it be convenient?**

Category 4: **I Don't Understand ...**
Please allow me to educate.

For every category you must have a response. So instead of having to learn many of them, **you only have to learn four.**

The four response correlators (second opinion, feel/felt/found, reschedule, and educate) are simply response thought triggers for you to use. When you completely articulate them, they could sound like this:

**Probe
Second Opinion**

Feel/Felt/Found

**a) To Talk:
Reschedule**

**b) To Implement:
Feel/Felt/Found,
Offer Pilot**

Educate

1. **No Need**

2. **Distrust**

3. **Inconvenience**

4. **Don't Understand**

1. No Need objection vs. Second Opinion response

*"Mr./Ms. Time Bandit, prior to my presenting you with the Time Locking proposal, I thought through the mutual benefits to you and me. What I'm asking is that you keep an open mind while you **allow me the opportunity to express my opinion** as to why I believe that Time Locking to overcome the adverse effect of interruptions will benefit you as much as me."*

Or, if you observed a need to reduce the Time Bandit's uncertainty or fear of the unknown about your Time Lock, you might say: *"I can see that this decision would be easier for you if you knew that my Time Locking would better meet your needs. Suppose we agree to my Time Locking this week, and next week we confer on whether I have indeed been able to provide you with better, more prompt, and higher quality service?"*

2. Distrust objection vs. Feel/Felt/Found response

*"I believe I understand how you **feel,** and I must admit that others in your position have **felt** the same way. However, they have **found** when they allowed me to explain how I would use Time Locking to benefit them, my firm, and my clients, they had no reason to distrust my intentions. If you enable me to Time Lock, I will prepare a step-by-step time-managed implementation action plan that can be easily tracked and quantified."*

Alternatively, you might say, *"Let's not make a full and permanent commitment yet, until we can prove to your satisfaction and mine that my Time Locking, and the time it frees up, will be put to good use. Let's settle now on the metrics we would use, and then revisit the concept after I complete two Time Locks."*

3. Inconvenience objection vs. Reschedule response

"I appreciate how busy you are, thus, if now is not a good time to get into detail, may I make an appointment at a more convenient time?"

If the Time Bandit displays concern over the inconvenience of installing Time Locking, offer to **pilot** Time Locking in **small increments** of time beginning with **just one half hour** and building from there.

4. I Don't Understand objection vs. Educate response

"I appreciate the fact that the Time Locking concept is a bold paradigm shift that, before implementing, needs to be thoroughly understood. What I'd like to do to better enable your understanding is present you with my step-by-step implementation action plan, which will in turn demonstrate all the benefits derived from Time Locking."

The next step to overcoming objections is to use the Objections Response Correlatators as a guide and brainstorm ideas, **in the third person only,** about how you would respond to each of the objections from each of your Time Bandits that you wrote down earlier. For example, *"Tell them that Time Locking will benefit them"* versus the actual script you will use.

> If the Time Bandit displays concern over the inconvenience of installing Time Locking, offer to **pilot Time Locking in small increments of time beginning with just one half hour.**

If you can face your fears and learn to overcome them, you will have removed most of the obstacles that circumscribe our lives.

To imagine a world without fear is to imagine a world of great people achieving great things. You don't have to be religious to know why one of the most common phrases in the Old and New Testaments is "fear not." Courage, peace, and strength come to those who fear not.

If we can overcome our fear of the unknown and the resulting fear of rejection, then we will have removed most of the obstacles that circumscribe our lives. There's no end to what you can accomplish. And now that you are fear-less, in the next chapter you will learn how to prepare your **first-person** personalized scripts for proposing Time Locking to your Time Bandits and, with a Dirty Harry attitude, overcome all of their predictable objections.

Go ahead, make my day!

5:30

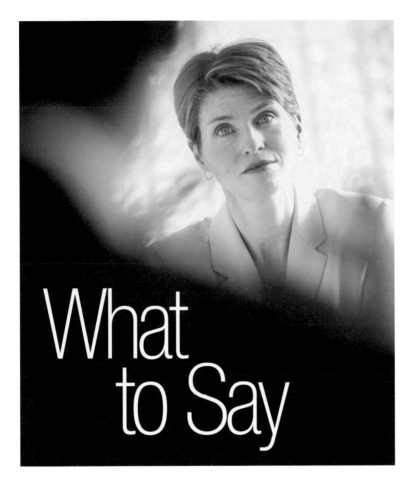

What to Say

Please do not just go "winging it" with your Time Bandits. **Remember what's at stake here –** nothing less than that precious, rare resource – **time.**

At this juncture, when I have completed the objections portion of STWM, our students are comforted, secure, and full of "make my day" self confidence. I can see that they are rarin' to go. They are saying to themselves, *"I'm ready. I get the idea – I can wing the rest!"*

Please do not, under any circumstances, just go "winging it" with your Time Bandits. Winging it is for bedtime stories and parlor games. Remember what's at stake here – nothing less than that precious, rare resource – time. Your Time Bandit interaction is one of the most significant conversations you might ever have.

The purpose of this chapter is to teach you how you can perform brilliantly during that critically important conversation when you present your Time Lock proposal to your Time Bandit – whether that's your clients, boss, or co-workers. You want to approach your Time Lock proposal so well-prepared that you are confident, professional, and able to adapt to whatever comes up in the conversation.

I learned the importance of scripting at a very young age, and have parlayed it across my entire career. I was still a teenager when I began my sales career to make money for my schooling.

That means thoroughly scripting exactly what to say, and thoroughly practicing exactly **how to say it.** This chapter will only cover the former – what to say. In Chapter 5:45, we will cover how to say it.

I learned the importance of scripting at a very young age, and have parlayed it across my entire career. I was still a teenager when I began my sales career to make money for my schooling. I sold everything – cash registers, vacuum cleaners, you name it. And I sold heating oil. Door-to-door. In the Bronx. In the summer!! Well before anybody had air-conditioned apartments. Seriously!!

You see, finding jobs was not so easy, and the only thing I could find one summer was selling heating oil to private homes. So, just think about it. It's August in the East Bronx and the temperature was between 80 and 90 degrees, and the humidity was equally high. Think about cold calling in a tough neighborhood. Here was my pitch:

"Mr. DeNapoli, I do hope I am not disturbing you on this very lovely Sunday."

He responds with:
"Hey, waddya mean lovely? You could fry an egg on the street it's so hot! Waddya want?"

To which I replied:
"Mr. DeNapoli, my name is Eddie Brown. The purpose of my visit is to help you save money, time, and aggravation."

He says:
"Yeah, waddya gonna do, get me some ice?"

I replied:
"No, I can't do that Mr DeNapoli, but what I can do is sell you heating oil at a huge discount."

You can imagine his response:
"Is this some kind of joke? It's 90 degrees, I'm in a pool of sweat, are you pazzi in testa? Why don't ya offer me one of those new Frigidaires?"

I calmly said to him:
"Mr. DeNapoli, do you remember what you went through last December? I know it's hard but can you remember that when you were ordering fuel oil, perhaps like everyone else in the neighborhood you were mad at Sunoco? You complained that the prices were too high and there was not enough oil to go around?

Just think about it, Mr. DeNapoli, if I were calling you in December with this same offer, you would be welcoming me into your home with open arms."

"Yeah, Yeah, but this ain't December!" he says.

"But Mr. DeNapoli," I said, *"my best customers are my smartest customers and they think ahead and they remember and like being able to tell their neighbors and their wives – 'See, I'm smart enough to think ahead.'"*

I know that I was only 16, and it may seem odd to you that a teenager would have thought of that presentation, but I didn't just wing it, I had a rehearsed 5-phase protocol that I will share with you later in this chapter.

You see, I knew that if I was to be successful selling anything, I would have to rely on more than charm. And if I was going to sell heating oil in August to sweltering New Yorkers, I had better know the right things to say. Correctly anticipating stolid resistance, I wrote down all the objections that I could think of plus those that I actually received from my first prospects.

Then I scripted a relevant and appropriate response for each predicted objection, one after the other. I practiced them over and over, making my parents and sister role-play as my prospects, refining my responses until they were as persuasive, articulate, and empathetic as possible, and I was able to deliver them with professionalism.

I know that I was only 16, **but I didn't just wing it,** I had a rehearsed 5-phase protocol that I will share with you later in this chapter.

When you're serving at match point, and your blood turns icy and you can barely lift your arm above your head, **what keeps you from double faulting are those thousands of practice serves.**

I know I must have been extremely diligent about this, because I recall my exasperated mother finally saying, *"If you don't stop pestering me with this, I am going to disown you. I've already purchased your vacuum cleaners, I don't need a cash register, and we live in an apartment and have no use for heating oil."*

But her patience and my preparation and practice paid off. I became Sunoco's number one sales professional.

Sure, I was probably somewhat lucky, but it was that experience of intensive practice that led me to firmly embrace, for the rest of my career, what others have concluded: *"We make our own luck."* Or, as the great American author and poet, Bret Harte, put it, *"Luck is what happens when preparation meets opportunity."* Ten thousand hours, according to Malcolm Gladwell's *Outliers,* is what it takes to master a skill: *"Practice isn't the thing you do once you're good. It's the thing that makes you good."*

All the practice and role-playing with my mom and sister didn't just help me deliver an effective performance. It also helped me to overcome all those fears we talked about earlier. I didn't want to be rejected. I didn't want to have to tell my family (and my 5-year-old self) that I had flunked at something. Sure, those are huge fears for teenagers, but let's not kid ourselves – they plague adults, too. Scripting and preparation put them to rest.

Rehearsal is nothing more than preparing yourself properly for the big moment.

Preparation and practice make you confident you can deliver no matter how difficult the conditions. When you're serving at match point for the Wimbledon trophy, and your blood turns icy and you can barely lift your arm above your head, what keeps you from double faulting are those thousands of practice serves. If you're a Navy SEAL and your helicopter crashes in the middle of a dangerous mission in enemy territory, you live or die depending on how well you prepared for such a contingency.

Scripting is a behavioral discipline designed to organize what you must develop and rehearse as a pre-condition for delivering a compelling and persuasive proposal. Actors learn their lines before going on the set. Soldiers check their weapons the night before. Chefs line up all the ingredients before they start. That's the reason you work on scripting.

Rehearsal is nothing more than preparing yourself properly for the big moment, so that the bigness of the moment doesn't overwhelm you.

When it comes to big moments in your work – and surely eliminating Time Banditry is big – *not* pre-scripting and

When it comes to big moments in your work – and surely eliminating Time Banditry is big – *not* pre-scripting and rehearsing would be unprofessional. It would be leaving to fate what you can and should control.

rehearsing would be unprofessional. It would be leaving to fate what you can and should control.

Scripting has a very precise, field-tested checklist that you must conform to, and once you do, I assure you that you will always feel prepared, organized, and confident in putting on your Time Locking (or for that matter, any other) presentation that you believe in.

Your Scripting Checklist

☐ **1. What are the key points you want to convey to the Time Bandit?** Just jot them down in the third person. For example, one point may be, *"Tell him this is for his benefit as well as mine"* (this is third person) – rather than *"May I propose an idea to you that would benefit both of us?"* (This is first person.)

☐ **2. What are the Big 5 headlines?**
Rank them in the order of priority.

1. _____

2. _____

3. _____

4. _____

5. _____

☐ **3. Now that you know your key points that are to be contained in your Big 5 headlines, please conform to these rules:**
- No hyperbole (truth only, please)
- Researched and factual
- Simple, clear and articulate
- Pre-position and encourage questions and objections
- Conversational (speak from the heart)

Your Scripting Checklist (continued)

4. Your list should contain the basic key elements:

- Although you are facing a critical deadline, you will help the Time Bandit with his/her needs.
- Explain the purpose and mutual benefits of your Time Locking goals and plans.
- Because of your current deadlines, seek concurrence for a formal in-person or telephone meeting time.
- Thank the client for his/her understanding and set the appointment.

Please personalize the Guideline Language that I have provided at the end of this chapter and in doing so, remember, the truth always wins and speak from your heart.

5. Rehearse, rehearse, rehearse.

- In STWM Scripting Clinics we depend on role-playing and reverse role-playing to perfect our presentations.
- If rehearsing with another is not an option, then the mirror becomes your best teammate.

6. Every professional sales presentation and/or artful negotiation contains five critically important phases. Below, I have custom-tailored those five phases for your Time Locking presentation to your Time Bandit. They are:

- Intro/Entry Lines
- Time Lock Solution Needs
- Response to Objections
- Exit Lines and Next Steps
- Time Lock Action Plan Close

In STWM Scripting Clinics **we depend on role-playing and reverse role-playing** to perfect our presentations. If you can't rehearse with another, then the mirror becomes your best teammate.

Any one of these (or variations of these) guideline Intro/Entry Lines will pre-position your next phase. How important is it to get these Intro/Entry Lines just right? Just recall the old cliché, *"There's no taking back a bad first impression."* Getting this right is essential.

Phase 1
Intro/Entry Lines

FORMAT	GUIDELINE LANGUAGE WITH **KEY ELEMENTS**
Greeting	● *Mr./Mrs. Time Bandit, I believe **I have found** a method for increasing my personal performance that will benefit both of us.* ● *Mr./Ms. Time Bandit, **(I believe) I have found the (mutually beneficial) solution for resolving** (your concerns over) my personal productivity and quality-control performance.* **OR** ● *Mr./Ms. Time Bandit, I believe I found a (mutually beneficial) solution for not only **meeting**, but **perhaps even exceeding**, (my/your) **productivity deadlines.*** **OR** ● *Mr./Ms. Time Bandit, I believe I have found a (mutually beneficial) solution for increasing and/or exceeding the quality of service performance that you require.* **OR** ● *As a result of **uncontrolled, unnecessary interruptions**, I've conducted a **productivity time loss self-analysis** and the quantitative (and qualitative) **adverse effects were astonishing.***

Phase 2
Time Lock Solution Needs

FORMAT	GUIDELINE LANGUAGE WITH **KEY ELEMENTS**
Explain Time Locking ● What it is ● Benefits to Time Bandit ● Benefits to you	● ***Time Locking for only** (one hour a day and/or 3 hours a week) can **increase** my **personal productivity by as much as (30%).*** ● *Mr./Ms. Time Bandit, if I were **empowered and enabled** to sustain even (2 hours, 5 hours, 1 day, etc.) a week of **uninterrupted time**, I believe I could **increase my quality-controlled productivity** by a factor of (10, 20, 50%).* ● *I believe without some form of **control over my unwanted, unneeded interruptions** such as Time Locking, **I'm wasting as much as** 30% or more of my (weekly, monthly, yearly) **productivity.***

> ● *I have read **a self-help book** entitled The Time Bandit Solution. TBS is based on a **proven, field-tested solution** entitled **Time Locking**. Depending on how much you Time Lock, **productivity can increase** by as much as 50% a week, month, or year.*

Phase 3
Response to Objections

It is here that you now apply what you learned in overcoming objections, Chapter 5:15.

FORMAT	GUIDELINE LANGUAGE WITH **KEY ELEMENTS**
For No Need, offer a second opinion **Use accurate empathy** ● Use the Feel, Felt, Found Principal **Educate about the...** ● Benefits to Time Bandit ● Benefits to you **Suggest a pilot**	● ***I understand how you feel.** Time Locking is revolutionary, not evolutionary.* ● *May I please give you my opinion of why Time Locking is as beneficial to you as it is to me?* ● *Were I in your position, I would **feel the same way** and question the Time Locking solution. However, I believe what **you will find,** if we were to agree to do this for a **pilot period** – perhaps three Time Locks – that Time Locking may be as important a **solution for you** and **your productivity needs as it is for me** and mine.* ● *Consider the fact that **my productivity increases benefit you** as much if not more than they benefit me.* ● *Here's why I believe once you look into the **cause and effect of interruptions,** you'll find **Time Locking logical,** sensible, beneficial, healthy, and necessary.* ● *There is **field-tested evidence,** from banks and companies in other industries, that the installation of Time Locking is **simple, cost-free, and immensely productive and profitable.***

Phase 4
Exit Lines and Next Steps

FORMAT	GUIDELINE LANGUAGE WITH **KEY ELEMENTS**
Present the proposal **Make mutual commitments**	● *Mr./Ms. Time Bandit, **thank you** for **considering** a **Time Locking** action plan proposal as a new way forward.* ● *I **propose** that I present you with a Time Locked Step-by-Step and Time-Managed **Implementation Action Plan.*** ● *May I propose an in-writing action plan:* ● *The action plan will contain a step-by-step **protocol.***

CONTINUED ON THE NEXT PAGE

CONTINUED FROM
THE PREVIOUS PAGE

● *There are 4 critical components to this protocol:* **What, Who, How Much, By When.**

  ● *By when does the Time Lock begin and end?*

  ● *What hours (days) will be our mutually-agreed-upon Time Lock?*

Phase 5
Time Lock Action Plan Close

FORMAT	GUIDELINE LANGUAGE WITH **KEY ELEMENTS**
Thank the Time Bandit for cooperating with you **Formalize the action plan** **Ask for any questions**	● *Mr./Ms. Time Bandit,* **thank you for your Time Lock cooperation and acceptance.** ● *Mr./Ms. Time Bandit,* **may I suggest** *how to* **proceed?** ● *Do you have* **any further questions** *and/or concerns? If not, may I suggest we both consider* **formalizing this action plan?**

These structures have been field-tested over and over and refined. They form the basis of a dialogue with your Time Bandit, rather than a monologue. A monologue turns into a dialogue if you simply pause between each of the five phases and ask for questions.

By asking for questions, you follow one of the important prerequisites of persuasion and selling which is (as we discussed) surfacing objections.

Here are some additional rules when your Time Bandit is a client:

When meeting your client at the appointment time, re-educate and reconfirm with your client how Time Locking will help you provide better service to him/her, and how much you appreciate your client's patience and understanding in agreeing to schedule the appointment. Ideally, when the client sees how carefully you address his or her issues during the appointment – because you've prepared yourself for this meeting – your client will appreciate your honesty, forthrightness, and skill in handling what might have been a difficult exchange.

Go over your script enough times so that you can say it through without referring to any notes. Practice it in front of the mirror until you can deliver it naturally.

Self Exercise in Scriptwriting

For the first part of this exercise, go back to your lists of Time Bandits and identify your major Time Bandit. Next, develop a first-person script for proposing your Time Locking needs, following the process we set forth above. Go over your script enough times so that you can say it through without referring to any notes. Practice it in front of the mirror until you can deliver it naturally. Prepare yourself for all predictable objections by remembering the four categories and the response correlators.

In writing your script, refer to the Guideline Language examples I shared with you in the five phases in the previous pages and **customize** your script to suit your own personality.

Now that you have prepared your Time Bandit scripts, in this next chapter we are going to go over the art of delivering those scripts with a style that will be honest, compelling, and from the heart, such that your presentation will be immensely credible to your Time Bandits and motivate them to accept your Time Locking plans.

CHAPTER

5:45

How to Say It

In the last chapter we learned the skill of *knowing what to say* to your Time Bandits when proposing Time Locking as well as when responding to any of their objections. Knowing what to say is the **skill** of communication. However, *knowing how to say what to say* is the **Art.** This chapter covers the artful component of Communications Arts and Skills which I simply call **Style.**

Cohen Brown's Communication Arts and Skills program creates the foundation for enhancing the ability to communicate with clients and prospects, thus achieving likeability, charisma, and credibility while seeking to satisfy their needs. The ability to articulate intelligently and gracefully increases self-confidence and self-esteem, and likewise reduces fear and anxiety.

Not only did the loss of my eye give me the drive to succeed, it also gave me a sense of survival. As I said before, I felt I had to do more and work harder in order to compete effectively in the normal-sighted world.

Knowing what to say is the skill of communica- tion. However, **knowing how to say what to say is the...**

Art

130

As I also said before, I grew up in the East Bronx where it was one rough neighborhood after another, and mine was particularly notorious. In those days it was not atypical in New York for each neighborhood to have a gang of kids stomping around, boasting, and threatening other gangs.

Even among the childish, yet dangerous hooliganism of gang-life, I found myself taking a leadership role in peacemaking. The right words seemed to come easily to me and always when I needed them, all of which presented me with a way to survive those days. I became known as the Great Negotiator. You can imagine that was a solace to me, still painfully self-conscious about my handicap and exaggerating its importance to others, as teenagers will do.

My pride in this skill – it was called "a gift of gab" back then – only grew as I discovered it could translate to school. I found myself competing not with gang members, but with academically accomplished students and even my teachers over better ways to articulate.

I've lived the truth of the proverb, *"It's not the events of life, but rather our perception of those events that shape our destiny."* It wasn't the accident, but the way I perceived my handicap and felt obliged to compensate for it, that caused me to become an effective communicator.

Likewise, when dealing with your Time Bandit, his perception of how you present your opposing point of view (when responding to objections) is going to determine whether he will be open and responsive versus defensive and frustrated.

Since your use and application of style begins with the delivery of your Phase 1 Intro/Entry Lines, your success will depend on how well you understand that what's important isn't just *what* you say, it's *how* you say what you say.

Even among the childish, yet dangerous hooliganism of gang-life, **I found myself taking a leadership** role in peacemaking. The right words seemed to come easily to me and always when I needed them.

Through all of my early experiences I came to understand that successful communication rests on eight basic style rules about the quality of your communication, all of which you must establish within the first 15–30 seconds of your opening salvo to your Time Bandit because there's no taking back a bad first impression.

Rule 1
Speak from the heart, not just the brain

One of the *stubbornest* fallacies we encounter is that sincerity can't be taught. If you don't feel it, you can only deliver your best facsimile. I sincerely disagree. Showing sincerity isn't a natural resource but a character trait. It is as learnable as any other virtue like empathy, respect, generosity, and kindness.

A former bank executive I knew when she was a young manager had to deal with a difficult customer. He was a law student who regularly tried to catch her staff on arcane compliance items, and he was abusive and profane to them. After one particularly egregious incident, she told him his business was no longer welcome and closed his account. That evening her regional manager called and said the customer was going to sue the bank because she hadn't given him proper warning. She was to re-open his account. *And* the customer was demanding that she personally apologize to him.

She did as asked, the apology unfelt but delivered with all the professionalism she could muster. But the customer still fumed, *"You don't sound like you mean it,"* and called her boss still threatening to sue.

That evening, her epiphany didn't come easily, but it came. She realized that from all the emotions surrounding the situation, she had to cultivate sincere regret and convey it to a bully, and do so convincingly. She had to put herself in his place, determine what he needed to experience,

Showing sincerity isn't a natural resource but a character trait. **It is as learnable as any other virtue** like empathy, respect, generosity, and kindness.

imagine what his behavior said about his emotional needs, and create that experience and those emotions. Her empathy was so sincere that what actually occurred was that the client was the one to apologize to her.

If you're going to deal with people, speaking from the heart, in order to sound credible, is an indispensable trait to cultivate. You see, in communication, credibility is the *sine qua non* of consultative persuasion, negotiating, and selling.

Additionally, when you respond to the Time Bandits, in the unlikely event that you hear, *"No, I'm not interested, I don't believe this will work in our environment,"* it's not enough to demonstrate empathy and credibility. You must also say what needs to be said without sounding robotic.

If you are on the phone and you sound robotic, the Time Bandit may assume you're reading a script.

A heartfelt presentation will not only make you sound credible, it will also make you sound likeable, which is very helpful when you are trying to get someone to do something new for you.

Rule 2
At all times, put a smile in your voice

There's truth in the adage that forcing a smile lifts your mood. Your smile changes your attitude and your voice. Science says that your smile triggers measurable activity in the area of your brain where happiness is registered. If just smiling makes you happier, how could the "sound" of your smile fail to have a salutary effect on the person hearing it?

Even over the phone, a smile can be detected and have an effect. It can calm fears, soothe anger, offer sympathy, soften resistance, and engender confidence. There are words that do this, too, but to be convincing they need to be reinforced and validated by a corresponding emotion in the sound of a smile.

Even over the phone, a smile can be detected and have an effect. It can calm fears, soothe anger, offer sympathy, soften resistance, and engender confidence.

133

What does that mean – a smile in your voice? The next time you get on the phone, no matter what your mood, literally smile. Now don't stop smiling until you're done making the primary point that you want to make. Then ask yourself if you felt better about how you communicated with the other person.

Rule 3
Use the correct tempo

So what is "Tempo"? In the context of communication style, the term "tempo" means the speed of speech. When listening to someone who speaks too fast, doesn't it feel like you are drinking from a fire hydrant?

Your voice should have **peaks and valleys.** Speak at a tempo that contains enough energy, as though you're really interested and enthusiastic, but is slow enough so that you're clear.

High-energy people speak too fast because, well, they have high energy. There is, however, the perception that fast talkers are insincere. Think of the stereotype of the used-car salesman. On the other hand, there is also the perception that people who speak too slow are dim-witted.

While I realize it's *"different strokes for different folks,"* nevertheless with respect to tempo, here's the rule:

Your voice should have peaks and valleys. Speak at a tempo that contains enough energy, as though you're really interested and enthusiastic but is slow enough so that you're clear. However, most importantly, always endeavor to match your tempo to that of the Time Bandit.

Rule 4
Use etiquette

I wish there were a different word for what I mean here. "Etiquette" has unfortunately taken on a connotation of pretension, or showy flourishes – something to be ridiculed, not emulated. I mean etiquette as a code of behavior based on respect and graciousness – a consistent demonstration of

respect and concern through words and actions – and even silences and inactions – that envelop the entire interaction.

When we teach Communications Arts and Skills, sometimes we get a little pushback about etiquette: *"That's not me – I think people prefer me to be 'real.'"*
I acknowledge that there is a time and place for that kind of "being real," but it's among friends and family, not with customers, the boss, or colleagues.

Although no one wants to feel as though we're utilizing an affectation to be unnecessarily polite, just practice on people you don't know and watch their reaction. After our participants try our etiquette approach, they quickly find themselves feeling more professional and in charge of the conversation. They also notice that customers and colleagues follow their lead. Polite behaviors lead to more politeness from others.

Utilizing etiquette always generates likability with just the simple use of what I refer to as "politeness superlatives," such as:

- *"Have you any questions?"*
- *"I do hope I was clear."*
- *"Thank you."*
- *"May I ask…"*
- *"That's very, very interesting."*
- *"Just to be certain, may I repeat what I believe you just said?"*

Superlatives not only convey the perception of respect but good upbringing and schooling as well. In a sentence it might sound like this:

"Thank you for answering my question. Before we go on, may I please repeat what you've said to make certain that I am perfectly clear? Thank you."

After our participants try our etiquette approach, they quickly find themselves **feeling more professional and in charge** of the conversation.

Arms aren't neutral or silent. Nothing scares a lecturer more than looking out at his audience and noticing **arms folded across their chests.** This body language is death.

The trick with the etiquette protocol technique is to use it without sounding patronizing. Avoiding this mistake is one of the major reasons that intense role-playing is so important. It is through role-playing that these etiquette protocol techniques are eventually woven into the tapestry of the way you communicate.

Rule 5
Utilize effective body language

What is body language? It is the story told by your physical posture, deportment, and gestures. Your body "speaks" even when you might think it's silent. It reveals you, and how you regard your situation, your companions, or the task at hand.

If you observe from a reasonable distance a conversation between two people, you will notice the way they compose and choreograph their body movements during the conversation. A trained professional who understands body language can know in an instant if someone is or is not:

- Telling the truth
- Fascinated
- Disinterested
- Passionate
- Arrogant
- Detached
- Listening
- Polite
- Bored

By studying behavioral expressions these professionals can literally discern intentions without listening to words. But is it only professionals who can read your body language? How about your spouse or your child, girlfriend, boyfriend, even a judge or jury?

Let's start with one of the most interesting body language examples. It's called "eye contact."

Eye contact doesn't mean staring down a client, friend, spouse, or child like a zombie. Eye contact should have flexibility, authenticity, and believability. Zombies don't have that. Zombies are scary. Your eyes and your face should move gracefully in relationship to what someone else is saying. They can close. They can open. But if you are telling a story and your eyes shift away from the other person, you look, well, shifty. You look as though you are lying, and the other person might well draw that conclusion.

It is said that the eyes are the mirrors of our soul. It is through these mirrors that we see ourselves and perceive our own personal incompetence and inadequacy, as well as our strengths.

Arms aren't neutral or silent. Nothing scares a lecturer more than looking out at his audience and noticing arms folded across their chests. This body language is death. It means, *"I don't like you, I don't trust you. I don't believe a word that you are saying, and I don't want to be here."*

Conversely, arms open, down, and/or to your side, means, *"I'm listening, I'm open, I like you, I trust you."* While listening to others, keep in mind what your arms say about you. And if you find yourself tapping your feet as you're listening, it could be construed as a sign of impatience.

And the number one body language offense? That would be yawning. It openly conveys what polite people conceal – boredom or disdain.

Rule 6
Use effective listening techniques

How hard can "good listening" be? Pay attention to what the other person says and don't interrupt, right?

Well, no. Effective listening is an active, participatory set of practices. One day I sat at sidewalk café and watched a person on the street give directions to a tourist. It was at once the most ordinary of interactions and at the same time an elaborate "pas de deux" of verbal, facial, and hand cues, quite aside from the actual directions which I could not hear. Tentative pointing, questioning looks, words repeated, firmer pointing, nodding, solicitude, gratitude, and finally smiles all around.

Effective listening is an active, participatory set of practices – an elaborate "pas de deux" of verbal, facial, and hand cues.

What I was watching was two people performing effective listening techniques as a matter of course. The local confirming where the tourist wanted to go, the tourist confirming the directions, the local elaborating, both of them quickly acknowledging the other's interjections.

But in too many conversations, there's silence when there should be acknowledgment. There's replying when there should be restating. There's interrupting and rushing. When that happens, people need to be trained in doing what those two did effortlessly on the street, and in adapting them to the particular needs – in this case the needs of the Time Locker and the Time Bandit.

To underscore this point further, remember the famous Hollywood icon, Clark Gable, who at the peak of his movie career was also at the peak of his popularity with women.

In an interview with Walter Winchell, Gable was asked, *"Clark, what is the secret to your success with women?"* Gable replied, *"Women think I'm the world's best conversationalist."* Winchell then asked, *"Clark, what does it take to become the world's best conversationalist?"* To which Gable responded, *"Knowing how to be the world's best listener."*

Rule 7
Visualize yourself being successful

To enable yourself to generate a positive attitude along with an enthusiastic, self-confident mindset, use the following Time Locking positive self-visualization and positive affirmation techniques:

- Visualize yourself completely composed, organized, service-driven, and productive.

- Visualize increased customer satisfaction based on your ability to provide increased service quality.

- Visualize management recognition based on increased high-quality productivity.

- Visualize management recognition for increased sales and service results that exceed management goals and expectations.

- Visualize management recognition for Time Locking innovativeness and originality.

- Visualize increased peer respect and peer Time Locking leadership.

- Visualize family and friends that you've wanted to spend more time with, grateful for your increased accessibility.

- While doing the foregoing visualizations use the following positive self-affirmation:

"Time Locking will satisfy everyone's needs including my own."

This positive affirmation means that if you can consultatively communicate all the mutual benefits of Time Locking to your interrupters, instead of being your Time Bandits, they will be converted into **time management friends and supporters.**

Rule 8
Role-play

To make sure you are applying each of the first seven rules to the best of your ability, role-play as I did with my mother and sister. This can be done alone or with a partner. As I said before, if you don't have a partner, use a mirror. A role-play enables you to develop self-confidence with poise, which in turn generates a sense of self-esteem and provides you with the self-motivation you need to take the risks associated with fear of rejection, fear of failure, and all other fears.

In other words, when you can walk away from a role-playing experience feeling that anxiety is no longer the price you will pay for your unprepared mind and mouth, then you are indeed prepared.

So now you have learned how to train all of your Time Bandits, right? There may be one more hiding in the weeds still thieving away at your precious time. Keep reading.

A role-play enables you to develop self-confidence with poise, which in turn generates a sense of self-esteem.

CHAPTER

6:00

Lurking in the corners of your subconscious is perhaps the most pervasive, dangerous, stubborn, and inflexible of all the Time Bandits.

Focal Locking

Let's consider the following hypothesis: you're all alone with Quiet Time. You have now made a deal with all your Time Bandits. They're happy, you're happy. No phones, no managers, no clients, no colleague interruptions.

You think to yourself, *"Despite this boatload of work and fast-approaching deadlines, without interruptions, no worries!"* You go on thinking, *"Now … now … I can build, maintain, and sustain momentum. I will increase my quality control, decrease my do-overs, restarts, and, without interruptions, I can literally recover 50% of the time that was wasted."* Sounds good? Is good!!

Sorry folks, it's not going to work.

Lurking in the corners of your subconscious, still thieving away, is perhaps the most invidious, pervasive, dangerous, stubborn, and inflexible of all the Time Bandits. He is the most frightening and the most challenging to overcome. This Time Bandit you really cannot arrest. Because he or she… is **YOU!**

You see, all the hard work you have just done dealing with your "external Time Bandits" would be a literal *"WASTE OF TIME"* if you did not Focal Lock and concentrate on the critical task at hand during your Time Lock.

"Focal Locking" is a term that we simply define as targeted focused concentration, or, in other words, *"Bearing Down"* with total focus to capitalize on and leverage the benefits of Time Locking.

The problem is that, as I said earlier, the Interruption Culture has fueled an Interruption Addiction, and it has been vastly exacerbated by the age of technology. Thanks to the Internet and its cyber-based progeny – Facebook, YouTube, emails, texts, smart phones, iPads, iPods – we are now bombarded by interruptions that would test the most focused, single-minded person.

Possibly our ancestors also succumbed to the appeal of interrupting their own hard work, too. Maybe spearhunters lying in ambush would tire, and start chatting to the hunter in the next cubicle, er... bush. Maybe Ben Franklin was taking a break and flying a kite for the fun of it. We know Nero turned to music when he should have been organizing bucket brigades.

Our personality types (as discussed in Chapter 3:00) also determine the nature of our Interruption Addiction. If you are a Type A, you *un*happily interrupt your Time Lock over and over because of your anxiety about all the *other* tasks you're neglecting when you Time Lock on just one. *"Let me just quickly return that one client call because I know she gets impatient. Oh, and then I should review that contract so I don't hold up my CFO. Okay, back to my Time Lock. Oh, I wonder if my hotel reservation was confirmed – better check on that..."*

If you're a Type C like my wife, you technically stay in your Time Lock, but it's ruined by the nagging knowledge that what you're doing has flaws or gaps. Type Cs find themselves consuming the Time Lock by perfecting its environment – a better lamp, a quieter fan, a cleaner desk – or by endlessly clarifying the objective so that they don't make a mistake. Type C writers find their writing flow sabotaged by a need to go back and shape the perfect sentence, fix the format, even find a better font.

If you are a Type B like me, you are so confident that you can get everything done, you happily interrupt your own Time Locks for new pursuits that float in over the transom: *"Of course, bring it in – no problem – I can finish this other task easily before my deadline."*

Possibly our ancestors also succumbed to the appeal of interrupting their own hard work, too. Maybe **Ben Franklin was taking a break** and flying a kite for the fun of it.

In 1890, William James, in his textbook *Principles of Psychology*, wrote, *"Concentration: It implies withdrawal from some things in order to deal effectively with others, and is a condition which has a real opposite in the confused, dazed, scatterbrained state."* Since the condition of interrupting ourselves is habitual, pervasive, and addictive, concentration requires more than just self-discipline. It requires a "Mental Paradigm Shift" from dispersed mind-wandering into targeted and focused concentration or "Focal Locking."

Focal Locking battles against the psychological and uncontrollable fact of life that all of us, at some level and to some degree, find that our minds wander, particularly when we are told, or we tell ourselves, to fully concentrate on the task at hand. We call this mind-wandering **Mental Leakage** and it's another big Time Bandit. When we lose our concentration to Mental Leakage, it feels like we are out of our control. But is it true – that we are at the mercy of this particular Time Bandit? No, but...

But we have to recognize that it is a powerful mental compulsion that makes Focal Locking most difficult at precisely the time we most need it. In fact, in the 21st century, an increasing portion of the world's population is diagnosed with some form of ADD (Attention Deficit Disorder) or ADHD (Attention Deficit Hyperactivity Disorder). Compulsive, as in addiction – we suffer from the overwhelming need to give in to a desire, that, despite the fact that we know that by doing so, we are sabotaging our higher intentions.

We are not masters of our own minds. We daydream. When what we're doing doesn't engage us tightly enough, our mind wanders to more attractive subjects – our next holiday, the coming weekend, what's for lunch. We worry. Will that big contract come through? What will the X-rays show? Are the kids getting a good education? Will I make it to the drycleaner before closing?

All of us find that our minds wander, particularly when we are told, or we tell ourselves, to fully concentrate on the task at hand. We call this mind wandering *Mental Leakage.*

Most people probably have some aspect of their job that tolerates no Mental Leakage. A brain surgeon in the operating theater would, we hope, be a good example. Or what about top athletes during competition, attorneys making their closing arguments, pilots at landing and take-off, or parents at critical character-forming moments in their children's lives? Even if you don't deal in matters of life and death, there is probably some part of your job where Mental Leakage is not an option.

Without Focal Locking we are vulnerable to **Brain Shutdown Phenomenon,** a condition common throughout our formative years in school. It simply means that for some reason we do not retain what our teachers tell us is critical to remember. It's as though the brain shuts down and refuses to absorb the data that we must retain.

Science helps us understand how we can improve our concentration. According to Richard Restak, MD, and his book, *Think Smart: A Neuroscientist's Prescription for Improving Your Brain's Performance,* "...thanks to advances in brain imaging techniques over the last thirty years, it's possible for neuroscientists to observe the development of the brain in real time. The imaging techniques show that blood flow to the brain varies with activity. The greater the activity, the greater the flow of blood needed to replenish the oxygen and glucose used by the active neurons."* The exercises in the next chapter will enable you to increase blood flow to the neurons which will, in turn, allow you to concentrate – to "Focal Lock" when you must and on what you wish.

Science also helps us understand that our brain works a lot like a computer.

That's why messages become encoded into our subconscious as well as our conscious minds. Mechanisms in the brain, where valuable and invaluable

Science also helps us understand that **our brain works a lot like a computer.** That's why messages become encoded into our subconscious as well as our conscious minds.

* Restak, Richard M. *Think Smart: A Neuroscientist's Prescription for Improving Your Brain's Performance.* New York: Riverhead, 2010.

Aunt Lettie's "trance" blocked out everything... What I saw as a trance is what I have redefined as **Focal Locking** – a deliberate tactic for accomplishing our goals without self-interruptions.

information is stored, enable us to act and react to information processing. The brain is like a muscle that trains itself to increase its information processing accuracy as it continues to do repetitive tasks. The faster we go, the more the brain is challenged to learn. The more the brain is challenged to learn, the stronger and better it gets at doing repetitive tasks accurately and quickly. When that happens, when we get a satisfying mental rhythm going, we call it *momentum*. When we are utilizing this kind of momentum, we are Focal Locked.

My Aunt Lettie knew how to Focal Lock. She worked part-time as a typist on a manual typewriter – her Smith Corona. No spell check. No back space. No autocorrect. She got paid by the page – by the *accurate* page. Mistakes were not tolerated.

When she was working, she was *focused.* She would have a cigarette dangling from her lips, the smoke would make her blink and cough, but she never stopped typing, and she never made a mistake. The more she typed, the faster she typed.

She would even close her eyes in concentration, and still those letters just flew out of her Smith Corona.

That was the first time I saw somebody make such a perfect marriage of the mind and the body, both functioning together, so synchronized that Aunt Lettie's house could have been on fire, the phones ringing off the wall, her children screaming, and her dog barking. But if Aunt Lettie had a deadline and sat down to meet that deadline, she would meet it no matter what.

When she was finished, she would take the cigarette from her lips, look around and scream, *"Who needs me, what the hell is going on around here, why doesn't anybody answer the phone?"* It was as though she were coming out of a trance. I asked her how she did that. She said, *"Eddie, I had a deadline to meet, and if I had to stop and think about what I was doing, I would hate what I was doing, I would make mistakes, and I would miss my deadline."*

Her "trance" blocked out everything that could lead to a distraction. What I saw as a trance then is what I have redefined as Focal Locking – a deliberate tactic for accomplishing our goals without self-interruptions.

Aunt Lettie has her modern-day counterparts in Warren Buffett and Bill Gates.

Seriously! I saw them interviewed on a talk show. They were asked, *"Warren, Bill, what self-discipline do you consider most contributed to your success?"* As though the two of them were Vulcan mind-melding, in unison they answered, *"Focus, Focus, Focus."*

But here's the really good news.
What Bill Gates, Warren Buffet, and my Aunt Lettie did, they perhaps did innately, but anyone can learn to do it. It can be

BUFFETT

GATES

What **Bill Gates, Warren Buffet,** and my Aunt Lettie did, they perhaps did innately, but anyone can learn to do it.

We have all had those experiences, like facing a looming exam, a crucial business decision, or a family illness, where it was blindingly evident that your full concentration was essential. When you crunched down and gave it your all, you were, without realizing it, **Focal Locking.**

our choice to either cave in to our own self-indulgent, personal interruptions and Time Banditry, or maintain our momentum through Time Locking and Focal Locking.

We have all had those experiences, like facing a looming exam, a crucial business decision, or a family illness, where it was blindingly evident that full concentration was essential. When you crunched down and gave it your all, you were, without realizing it, Focal Locking.

To start your Focal Locking mastery let's begin by determining whether or not you suffer from the effects of Mental Leakage so please take the following quiz:

No Mental Leakage Quiz

Estimate what is the longest "No Mental Leakage" Focal Lock amount of time you believe you can currently achieve without any further training? In other words, no phone interruptions, no television, no email or texts, no thinking about anything other than the task at hand.

1. 10 minutes?

2. Half an hour?

3. Two hours?

4. Three hours?

When you do get distracted, how long does it take you to re-focus on the task at hand?

1. Half an hour?

2. 15 minutes?

3. 5 minutes?

4. No time at all?

How many times during the exercise did you become distracted?

1. Four times

2. Three times

3. Two times

4. One time

What did it take to get you to focus again?

1. Did you decide that you could do it another time?

2. Did you have to take a break?

3. Did you remember the negative consequences of not getting the task done?

4. Did you simply tell yourself, *"Focus"?*

The
concept
amounts to
a grownup
version of
the rule my
mother
instituted
when I
started first
grade:
**Finish
homework
first, and
then you
can play
outside.**

**If the sum
of your
answers**
did not equal
at least 8, I'm going
to assume that you found,
as my students find when I teach
this, that Mental Leakage is a worse
Time Bandit than you had expected.

Einstein once said that the
definition of lunacy was to do the same
thing and expect a different result. As I
have for years understood, as writer Brian
Alexander explained in an article for *More*
magazine entitled "Change One Small
Habit, Change Your Life":

*"Simply plug new routines into your day
and stick with them until they become
habits. The concept amounts to a
grownup version of the rule my mother
instituted when I started first grade:
Finish homework first, and then you
can play outside. The bigger payoff
is that these new habits can, in turn,
become 'keystones' supporting other,
seemingly unrelated changes. Change
one habit, and maybe your social life will improve, your business
will become more profitable, your family will be happier.*

*"The idea is simple to state but not so simple to put into practice.
If rebooting our habits were easy, 'we'd all be thin, and we
wouldn't have so many people with drinking problems,' says
Dartmouth University Professor Todd Heatherton, PhD, who
researches self-regulation, the process by which people exert
control over their behavior. Still, habits form according to an
elegantly simple logic, and understanding the process opens the
door to all sorts of beneficial changes.*

"Your brain loves it *when you develop habits. That's because
your brain requires lots of energy, especially when you're reasoning,
so the more activity it can shunt onto autopilot, the more power it
has for complicated stuff like completing your tax returns. To keep
you from having to think about behaviors you repeat often – how
you commute to work, take a shower, make love – your brain forms
sets of boilerplate instructions.*

"How does the brain persuade us to embrace a habit? By giving us rewards (through a series of chemicals that activate pleasure and motivational circuits), it teaches us to always respond to a certain cue with the same routine behavior. For example, you see that it's 7:30 AM (cue), so you hop into your car and drive to work (routine). Because you've left on time, you avoid traffic and get to work exactly when you should (reward). A cue could also be the sight of your favorite chocolate. Eat the chocolate (your 'routine' whenever you see a tasty-looking piece), and your pleasure circuits will spring into high gear. Another example: Your beloved gets home from work (cue), and you sit down to drink dirty martinis together (routine). Eat, drink, have [fun] – in every case, your brain chemicals will provide bliss or, even more powerfully, release you from stress or anxiety. When we get a reward, we're motivated to repeat whatever action (routine) led to it. Soon we're in what [the author of The Power of Habit, Charles] Duhigg calls a habit loop. His equation:*
cue + routine + reward = habit.

When we get a reward, *we're motivated to repeat whatever action (routine) led to it. Soon we're in what Duhigg calls a habit loop. His equation:* **cue + routine + reward = habit.**

149

*My leisurely morning routine – **reading the newspaper for hours over coffee and breakfast before sitting down at my keyboard** – resulted in my accomplishing far too little in a workday.*

"Many of our habits – of our habits – often the bad ones – are formed as a result of our efforts to relieve tension or anxiety. Sharon Rowe, 56, an entrepreneur in Ossining, New York, cofounded Ecobags.com, a pioneer in the reusable-bag industry. Like many other small-business owners, she felt constantly on call, hypervigilant for any sign of a snafu. 'The sound of an incoming e-mail or text was my cue,' she recalls. 'When I did not have my phone, I was anxious, and when I did have it, I was constantly checking it.' Her routine was to interrupt whatever she was doing to check the screen. Her reward was either the satisfaction of a pleasant social connection (one of the most powerful human cravings) or the release of anxiety that comes from knowing she had headed off a work problem. But her habit became 'an overwhelming time suck,' she says, and it annoyed her friends.

"In trying to change my work life, I too had to deal with a 'time suck' habit. I've known for years that my leisurely morning routine – reading the newspaper for hours over coffee and breakfast before sitting down at my keyboard – resulted in my accomplishing far too little in a workday. But like Rowe, like everyone else, I've been caught in a battle between reward and reason, a struggle in which our reward circuits have the

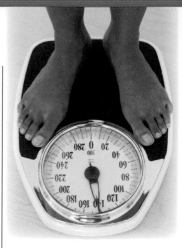

advantage. Located primarily in our midbrain, reward circuits developed early in evolution to drive us to seek food, water and sleep and to reproduce. Likewise, fear and anxiety circuits, also extremely powerful motivators, evolved early so we'd try to escape danger. But our rational circuits, centered mainly in the pre-frontal cortex (PFC), behind our foreheads, evolved much later. They help us look into the future and anticipate the consequences of our actions. We use our rational circuits to calculate risk, make complex decisions, exert self-control – and help us form positive habits. Every time a dieter is confronted with a double-cheese pizza, reward circuits shout 'Yes!' while the rational brain shouts 'No!' In my case, every time my alarm goes off at 5:30 in the morning, my PFC says 'Get up, get up!' but my reward circuits say 'Noooo! More sleep!'" *

To win the battle and overcome the cue-routine-reward loop, I want to share with you a process-driven methodology that I've developed for overcoming the Mental Leakage compulsion phenomenon and thus achieve Focal Locking. The name I've given to this methodology is **The Mental Hygiene Process** and it is the topic of our next chapter.

* Alexander, Brian. "Change One Small Habit, Change Your Life." More.com
www.more.com/relationships/attitudes/change-one-small-habit-change-your-life

*Every time a dieter is confronted with a double-cheese pizza, **reward circuits shout "Yes!"** while the rational brain shouts "No!"*

CHAPTER

7:00

I don't think I would have survived without the Mental Hygiene Process providing me the ability to Focal Lock.

The Mental Hygiene Process

I had a harrowing experience that I don't think I would have survived without the Mental Hygiene Process providing me the ability to Focal Lock. So harrowing that, as I start writing this story, I feel myself drawing the deep, anxious breaths of a trapped claustrophobe.

I was scuba diving, and delighted that my wife was finally joining me. Her mild discomfort with breathing through the regulator would cause her to remove her mask from time to time, and we would have to surface more swiftly than safety would dictate. Divers, climbers, and air travelers know that too-rapid changes in air pressure can cause physiological damage, colloquially known as "the bends," and technically as nitrous oxide poisoning. Severe enough, it kills.

I knew the symptoms, thankfully, and when I experienced them after a particularly rigorous day of diving, took myself to the emergency room. What I didn't know was the treatment. The ER doctor was swift with the prescription – *"You need to be in a decompression chamber, right now!"*

Fine. I wasn't thrilled – who would be? I knew what a decompression chamber looked like: a human-sized can. Who would want to submit to that? But I was in enough pain and aware enough of the danger of my condition that I was compliant.

"How long will I be?" I asked, already regretting how this trip to the hospital had wasted an hour of a beautiful Florida day.

His answer chilled me. *"Nine hours."*

If you have ever received frightening news, maybe you recognize my first emotion. It was simple. *"I cannot do this."* No more claustrophobic than the ordinary person, I still couldn't imagine being confined to a barely see-through coffin for much longer than I could hold my breath. Nine hours!!! That's driving clear across Texas! That's flying from New York to Berlin! That is a whole working day with nothing to do but think in a situation where all thoughts are terrifying. I would panic. I would suffocate. If I screamed would they hear me? Help me? All those thoughts raced through my mind as it had joined my body in torturing me.

The doctor was waiting, more stern-looking than sympathetic. This obviously wasn't his first time having to frighten somebody into saving their own life at the risk of their sanity.

His firmness helped, actually. I remember clenching my fists as if to physically regain control of my mind, and telling him one of the biggest lies I've ever told in my life: *"I'm ready."*

I wasn't, but I knew I had to get ready and fast. *"Can't"* is meaningless when death is the only alternative. I had to get to *"can"* before they closed the lid on that chamber.

That's when my old friend, the inner five-year-old spoke up – the same proud, injured child who had vowed to show the world. This time he vowed to survive. *"If living depends on being clamped inside a Lucite-lidded tube, well, that's what we'll do,"* he as much as told me.

Obviously I survived, or I wouldn't be writing this book. But what enabled me to get through it? I drew on almost everything I had ever learned in my whole life in order to grant myself an out-of-body experience. Seriously. I had to accomplish things with my mind over the strenuous, panicky objections of my body.

No farmwife can lift a tractor off her injured husband, but it happens with amazing frequency. No self-preserving human being runs into a fire and comes out with the baby, but it's commonplace in the news. And I believe people when they say later, *"I wasn't being a hero, I just had to do it."* I'm not comparing myself to heroes – I'm just saying *"had to"* trumps *"can't"* all the time.

As they lowered the lid on me, I realized that all of my historical survival instincts were going to be tested during the next nine hours.

No self-preserving human being runs into a fire and comes out with the baby, but it's commonplace in the news. And I believe people when they say later, *"I wasn't being a hero, I just had to do it."* I'm just saying ***"had to"* trumps *"can't"* all the time.**

153

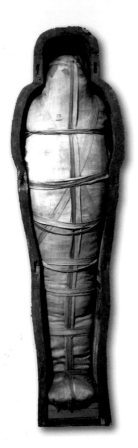

So there I was, encased like a mummy but able to exercise my life's lessons in the form of **Psychological Martial Arts** to battle against the incipient panic, claustrophobia, and mental deprivation of my cocoon.

I tapped into every available aspect of my soul and my brain. My first mental move was to reach for Constructive Acceptance – that is, to accept what had to be and make the best of it. It took some striving but I managed it.

Then I strove to recognize this current reality as a fresh form of Quiet Time – to welcome it the same way I normally welcome my solitude when I desperately needed it. But when my mind balked at being told to ignore the Lucite tube and instead visualize my ocean-view den or my rose-filled garden, I realized I would need something stronger – I would need some form of what I call **Psychological Martial Arts.**

Fortunately, I had been studying *hatha yoga* – a holistic form of yoga that encompasses discipline, posture, purification, gestures, breathing, and meditation. I had also learned *Ujjayi breathing* – a type of Pranayama breathing – a practice that brings bliss with little expenditure of energy or motion, which was useful given my severe confinement. The fact that Ujjayi is sometimes called Conquer Breathing cheered me up as I knew I had to win this bout and suppress my fears or risk my life. I had also come away with many techniques from my fruitful association with my partner, Marty, which provided me the knowledge to teach and train self-motivational and psychotherapeutic techniques.

Confined to my chamber, I was grateful for every method I could recall, even though I had rarely practiced them for more than 15 or 30 minutes, far short of my nine hour ordeal.

So there I was, encased like a mummy but nevertheless able to exercise my life's lessons in the form of Psychological Martial Arts to battle against the incipient panic, claustrophobia, and mental deprivation of my cocoon.

It was rough at first – one Positive Affirmation, then two panic attacks, then one *Ujjayi* breaths followed by two anxious gulps, and so on, with claustrophobia nibbling around the edges of my psyche. Slowly but surely I reached a delusional state – like, I suppose, the farmwife who believes she can lift a tractor, or the stranger who believes he should rush into a burning house. My body was still encased in that tube, but my mind rose up and visited the cosmos. From somewhere in the universe, I looked down and saw me lying there. I saw the stratosphere, the atmosphere, the stars, the planets. And I kept my mind floating there for hours before I chose to come down and rejoin it with my body.

Another extraordinary – and extremely positive – thing happened to me in that state in that chamber. At the time, my mother was dying of cancer, and I was really struggling to cope with that while I had a lot of employees and clients and other family depending on me. During those nine hours, thoughts of my mother would intrude into my meditation, but not in a stressful way. Gentle images would brush against my consciousness, and I would leave the cosmos, acknowledge my imminent loss, and then return to my suspended state. I don't pretend to understand exactly how that happened, but when it was all over, I had accepted my mother's situation with more calmness than I could ever have prayed for.

When I did return to terra firma for good, I realized I had, in the least hospitable circumstances, developed my customized form of meditation that allowed me to transcend my situation. Talk about turning lemons into lemonade! I also realized that my confinement in the chamber was another form of Quiet Time – not as desirable as the places I usually sought out for Quiet Time, but obviously just as productive. And so I embarked on regular use of a series of exercises as the source of my empowerment and enablement for so many different challenges. Ultimately, when I used these exercises to tame my own internal Time Bandit, I dubbed the practice the **Mental Hygiene Process.**

Just the phrase "Mental Hygiene" tells you its essential nature. You wouldn't think of getting up in the morning without washing your hands, brushing your teeth, and showering, would you? You want this Mental Hygiene Process to become as habitual and natural as the physical hygiene process, so that you will, without giving it a thought, automatically incorporate its various techniques.

The Mental Hygiene Process has very defined, learnable skills, and includes

You want this Mental Hygiene Process to become as habitual and natural as the physical hygiene process, so that you will, without giving it a thought, automatically incorporate its various techniques.

a series of proven, researched techniques and exercises specifically designed for the purpose of increasing sustained behavioral peak performance through concentration – that is, Focal Locking. In fact, as you will come to learn, this process more than just controls Mental Leakage, it is also designed to resolve the causes and effects of distress because when it is integrated into your life holistically, it will provide you with continuous feel-good energy.

For the purposes of this book, I draw from six of Cohen Brown's nine **Highest Correlators of Psychotherapeutic Techniques**:

1. Transcending the Environment
2. Constructive Acceptance
3. Visualizing the Ideal Self
4. Positive Affirmation
5. Psychological Counterpunching
6. Changing Your Internal Computer Chip

In addition there is the ultimate psychotherapeutic solution, **Focal Locking Martial Arts.** The primary objective of Focal Locking Martial Arts is the transformation of Mental Leakage causes and effects into a completely relaxed and focused state of mind, which is achieved through meditative relaxation while incorporating the six techniques as well.

The Six Techniques of the Mental Hygiene Process

Technique 1: Transcending the Environment

Transcending the environment is to rise above physical issues that you cannot change. Consider the air conditioning in your facility. How many of you have been in an office where the air conditioning failed in the summer? Now, if you spent your time thinking, *"Oh, the air conditioning is down, and I'm sweating. It's ruining my shirt, and it's too hot,"* you increase your discomfort by focusing on the heat.

But if you distract yourself from the heat, not only do you decrease your

> All it takes is for you to remove your mind from the source of the suffering and instead **focus on something pleasant** or innocuous.

discomfort, but you're functional. All it takes is for you to remove your mind from the source of the suffering and instead focus on something pleasant or innocuous. You have to keep cool in the face of the fact that the lack of air conditioning is making you physically warm. You are not a thermometer, obliged to rise when it's hot and drop when it's cold.

There are also other environmental issues you cannot change, like the company's administrative, operations, and compliance policies. You may want to help a customer over certain hurdles, for example, but given the compliance policies, the customer simply doesn't qualify. You are bound by policies that are beyond your control. Given that you have no control over these things, sometimes you have to learn how to transcend the environment by utilizing **Constructive Acceptance.**

Technique 2:
Constructive Acceptance

Constructive Acceptance means accepting that which you cannot change and doing so graciously, not grudgingly. I had my own struggle learning this one.

When I was seventeen, I was a good basketball player with a dream to play in the NBA and a chance at a basketball college scholarship. I could play power forward and guard, but I wanted to be a center. I was only 6'2" while Wilt Chamberlain, a contemporary of mine, was already 7'2". However, I thought I could still grow or else be the shortest and most effective center in the history of basketball. It wasn't to be. It wasn't in my DNA. And I didn't want to compromise. I didn't want to play forward or guard. So guess what? I never got that scholarship, and I was always sorry.

What I needed to learn, and I eventually did, was Constructive Acceptance. I had to transcend my particular physiological shortcoming – I simply wasn't tall enough to play center, and I needed to accept what was beyond my power to change.

Technique 3: Visualizing the Ideal Self

What I'd like you to do is visualize yourself in a Focal Lock when suddenly a negative thought or distraction comes into your mind. When that happens, I want you to replace it with a positive thought or idea.

What I needed to learn was Constructive Acceptance. I had to transcend my particular physiological shortcoming **– I simply wasn't tall enough to play center** – and accept what was beyond my power to change.

It's as simple as this: if I say, *"Don't think about a pink elephant,"* and you say, *"That's impossible,"* I say, *"Well, if you can think about a pink elephant, now think about a mountain instead."* Notice how quickly the mountain replaced the elephant?

One affirmative technique I use to transcend environmental challenges that I cannot change is to visualize my ideal self as a winner in a given situation. The premise is that if you can see what it would be like for your ideal self to transcend a challenge, and if you could then inhabit your ideal self, you would be able to Focal Lock with complete success. It means visualizing yourself successful with all the goals you hope to achieve despite challenges, conflicts, and adversity.

Visualizing the ideal self should be just part of getting ready for game day, even if game day is every day as it is for many of us. It's just Mental Hygiene.

Great athletes pump themselves up before a competition by visualizing themselves winning. Attorneys do it before they go to trial, and business executives giving critical presentations prepare the same way. I do visualizations before each lecture I give in the best way that I can. I visualized myself succeeding in putting this manuscript together, and I visualized what success would look like.

Visualizing the ideal self should be just part of getting ready for game day, even if game day is every day as it is for many of us. It's just Mental Hygiene.

Technique 4: Positive Affirmation

"I can do it!"

"Every day when I wake up," the popular psychologist and pharmacist Emile Coué said, *"in each and every way I'm going to feel better and better and better."* That used to sound just silly to me. Not useful, just silly. I thought the same thing when I first heard the Nike positive affirmation commercial, *"Just Do It."* Simplistic and silly.

But I gamely gave it a try, and was converted. Now, whenever I use my version, *"I can do it,"* my first intention is to program my subconscious mind through conscious thought to think positive. My second intention is to give myself an adrenaline rush. When you get a positive thrust in your mind from a phrase, it's back to the concept of Pavlovian conditioning. The mental causes the physical. It is a "trigger." I am actually stimulating adrenaline release in my body. Because by now I have paired the feeling of the adrenaline rush with a phrase such as *"I can do it,"* whenever I start saying that phrase, I start the blood flowing.

It doesn't happen overnight, of course. And yes, at first it might sound a bit silly. But it's worth staying with it to give it a chance to develop meaning and utility. Give it time to establish a connection between the physical and the mental. The whole idea is to charge yourself up. For me, *"I can do it"* works. A friend likes to say, *"I LIKE this"* until she does. You will find what works for you if you give it a little time.

Technique 5:
Psychological
Counterpunching

Let me give you another technique that is very effective for replacing a negative mindset with a **positive affirmation.** It's called **"Counterpunching."**

In the 1960s, one of the world's great all-time heavyweight champions, Muhammad Ali, was best known for his ability to counterpunch. Counterpunching is more than just punching back, trading punch for punch. It is *"the art of making him miss, then making him pay. A good counterpuncher will hit without being hit. But just as importantly, he can make the opponent so scared to throw a punch that his offense dissolves away, leaving him gun-shy and helpless."**

Ali would talk about a number of techniques such as *"flying like a butterfly and stinging like a bee"* but counterpunching was his real forte. Here is how you can use the counterpunching technique as part of your Mental Hygiene.

* "C is for." Boxing A-Z. http://marviningram.blogspot.com/2012/04/c-is-for.html

Counter-punching is effective for replacing a negative mindset with a **positive affirmation.**

The human brain is like a computer memory chip. Once a pattern has been embedded into that computer chip, we must do something different to change it.

1. Think of yourself as Muhammad Ali.

2. Your Mental Leakage Time Bandit throws a **negative** affirmation right cross. **He says:** *"No you can't finish that project, you are getting tired."*

3. You block the right cross with your **first** positive affirmation left cross. **You say:** *"Yes I can."*

4. Ultimately, you knock out your opponent with a **second** positive affirmation right uppercut. *"Just do it."*

Negative affirmation: right cross

First positive affirmation: left cross

Second positive affirmation: right uppercut

Technique 6: Changing Your Internal Computer Chip

As I said, the human brain is like a computer memory chip. Once a pattern has been embedded into that computer chip, we must do something different to change it. It is not enough to simply say stop doing a negative behavior. This means that for the Mental Hygiene Process to work, you must replace an old behavior with a new behavior. Let me give you an example.

While attempting to learn to play golf, I would slice the ball way off to right and generally into the rough or the trees. My friends watching me play would say, *"You are lifting your head."* By lifting my head, the face of the club would not make contact with the ball at the "sweet spot." I would hear the same advice over and over again, *"Keep your head down."*

But the memory chip in my brain, the muscle memory if you will, would not let me do it. The chip would tell me to look up to see where the ball went.

Out of frustration,
I hired a golf pro to help me. He placed a penny next to the ball and said, *"Don't take your eye off the penny. Concentrate through your entire swing staring at the penny and not at the ball. Your shoulder will naturally pick up your head at the end of the swing."* I tried it and I hit a ball a straight as I could ever have hoped for.

So what actually occurred? It simply was not enough to say, *"Don't pick up your head."* I needed something different to be programmed into my memory chip. Staring at the penny was the new program.

By practicing this over and over again, you can create a new memory chip in your brain. You must do the same thing every time you lose focus so that your new memory chip will allow you to relax and visualize yourself successfully completing the task with positive affirmations.

The advice? *"Keep your head down."* But the memory chip in my brain would not let me do it. The chip would tell me to look up to see where the ball went.

Focal Locking Martial Arts

Now that you have a way of giving yourself positive energy, the next step in the Mental Hygiene Process is to put yourself in a calm state of mind as I did in the decompression chamber. For this we have **Focal Locking Martial Arts.**

Focal Locking Martial Arts has a protocol. The protocol calls for the use and application of meditative relaxation through stillness, utilizing exercises built around what the East Indians define as meditation achieved through Pranayama breathing.

To put
yourself in
a calm state
of mind,
we have
**Focal
Locking
Martial Arts.**

"Pranayama" is the Sanskrit word for *"breath of life."* It is the reason yogis focus on not just breathing but how to breathe, how to inhale, and how to exhale. Our life is in our breath.

Several meditation and relaxation techniques have proven to decidedly improve cognition, quality of life, and personal happiness. Some users have even been able to overcome the effects of migraine headaches and other such maladies.

The gurus of East India believe that when the mind is still and empty of all distressful thoughts, feelings, or impressions, "moments of bliss" actually occur between the inhalation and exhalation of breath.

In this Focal Locking Martial Arts exercise for which you're about to receive specific instructions, each step is designed to empty your mind of all sources of Mental Leakage (whether distressful or joyful); if they invade your Focal Lock, they're unwelcome.

Once your mind is empty of all thoughts and thus Mental Leakage, only positive self-images, in combination with the mantra you will learn, will materialize in your mind. When this moment occurs, I believe you'll find your own source of bliss and focus.

To get started with Focal Locking Martial Arts, please follow these carefully defined instructions:

1. Find an ordinary four-legged chair with a hard back.

2. Remove your shoes; take inventory of your entire body by first noticing your ankles, your toes, and your fingers.

3. Rub your fingers together, move your toes. What you're seeking to do is warm up your extremities. You're seeking to notice that you're more than just a brain. You have a back, you also have hair, arms, a lower back, and so on.

4. Relax all of them as best as you can, even prior to proceeding with any form of relaxation and calming exercise.

(While you're first doing this exercise – reading it and carrying out the steps alone without a leader talking you through the steps – you may find it less than ideal. But carry on so that once you learn this exercise as I have, meditating alone anywhere you like at any time is not only achievable, you may find it preferable as I do.)

CALM

5. Now please close your eyes and just breathe normally. Use a mental mantra I simply call *"Calm."* A mantra is a sound, syllable, word, or group of words that is considered capable of "creating transformation." Yogis have used a mantra as a means of enabling focus. For this reason, I cannot think of a better mental mantra than the word *"Calm."* Yogis teach us that when we inhale, bringing oxygen into our lungs increases energy. On the other hand, exhaling increases relaxation.

6. With your eyes closed, slowly, slowly, inhale. Fill your lungs with as much oxygen as is comfortable.

7. Now, just as slowly, slowly exhale. On the exhalation, staying focused on the mantra *"Calm,"* say the word *"Calm"* softly out loud. As you do, you will feel calm coming over you. You will be absorbed and undistracted.

Now that you see how meditation works, believe me when I tell you you're on the road to becoming a black belt in Focal Locking Martial Arts.

This next task builds upon what you've just experienced and is designed to deepen your meditative relaxation results and, in doing so, help you increase the capacity to achieve Mental Leakage-free Focal Locking.

8. As you continue relaxing in your chair, breathing quietly, visualize that your breath has two colors – blue and gold.

Implemented correctly, these steps will empty your mind from the causes and effects of Mental Leakage.

Warm

Cool

When you inhale the **warm gold color,** the air you inhale will rest on the central vortex of your brain (which East Indians gurus refer to as the "third eye").

9. Focusing on your inhalation, press your right thumb on your right nostril to close off the right nostril airway and commence slowly inhaling warm golden air through your left nostril.

10. Now, focusing on your exhalation, do the opposite by lifting your right thumb off your right nostril and pressing on your left nostril with your right hand forefinger. Visualize that the air you exhale is an azure, cooling blue color.

When you inhale the warm gold color, the air you inhale will rest on the central vortex of your brain (which East Indians gurus refer to as the "third eye"). It is in the vortex of your brain that the color yellow transposes into blue and your exhalation of the blue breath is completed. Energized and relaxed through the inhalation of your golden breath, it is during the exhalation of that same cooling breath (now turned blue) that you begin to focus on your mantra.

Implemented correctly, these steps should have emptied your mind from the causes and effects of Mental Leakage. The next step will now fill your mind with combinations of the positive *"Calm"* mantra with a positive visualization such as the cosmos, a beautiful restful seascape, or landscape.

An alternative to a generic visualization is a very personalized visualization such as your interpretation of success, good health, etc. When I asked a colleague of mine for her selection of positive visualizations, she told me that hers would be the joy she feels when visualizing her eight grandchildren. It makes no difference which visualization you select, so long as it makes you feel joyful and positive. Below please find a list of typical personalized self-visualizations offered by various colleagues of mine.

- Meeting/exceeding goals, aspirations, and dreams
- Distress-free life
- Increased management/employer recognition
- Increased family love and recognition
- Increased physical and psychological health and welfare
- Increased overall happiness
- An overall positive mental attitude that, prior to meditative relaxation, was heretofore negative

Whether or not it takes you one or several inhalations and exhalations, the entire exercise will continue to increase your sense of well being, blissful concurrent high energy and relaxation. Remember, this technique is thousands of years old.

When you complete and have repeated this Mental Leakage avoidance exercise two or three times, the mantra, *"Calm,"* will have been consciously and subconsciously embedded such that you can call upon your mantra to become your how-to psychological Focal Locking trigger at will.

Now, imagine using this relaxation and calming exercise to start your day, end your day, and even refresh yourself in the middle of your day. You can use your mantra as a trigger to regain concentration every time Mental Leakage rears its ugly head.

The next step will now fill your mind with combinations of the positive *"Calm"* mantra with a positive visualization such as **the cosmos, a beautiful restful seascape, or landscape.**

There was a time when these techniques might have seemed unusual, but in today's connected world, Eastern methods and medicine have been embraced everywhere, even in areas that used to be stiff and skeptical about them. Yoga, for example, once largely confined to pockets in our society, has gone mainstream with millions of devotees, including athletes and business professionals, as well as people from all walks of life.

Now, imagine **using this relaxation and calming exercise** to start your day, end your day, and even refresh yourself in the middle of your day.

Since the entire purpose of the Mental Hygiene Process is to overcome the cause and effect of Mental Leakage, unbundle the process and pick and choose only what you need to regain Focal Locking control. At times you may find yourself needing counterpunching in combination with a positive affirmation, along with positive self-visualization, but not necessarily feel the need or desire to use **Focal Locking Martial Arts.**

The Mental Hygiene Process is a quiver of Mental Leakage self-defense arrows. Use them as needed and, to gain Focal Locking control, shoot them accurately.

Now that you have the tools to Focal Lock within your Time Lock, it is time to ask, what are the tasks that we should concentrate on during the Time Lock? This next chapter will help you leverage the time you have just recovered from your Time Bandits beginning with learning how to determine what's critical and what's not.

Time Gained
Behavioral Planning

In the Time Gained Behavioral Planning section you will learn how to keep the promises you have made to your Time Bandits and utilize the time recaptured through Structured Time-Managed Behavioral Planning, the pathway for implementing all of your critical initiatives and tasks.

™

80/20 Critical Few Planning

"Life is what happens to you while you're busy making other plans."

— JOHN LENNON

You have now learned how to wrest your own time back from your Time Bandits, including the most persistent of all – *you.* You have made others comfortable with your Time Locks. But you didn't do all that so that time could hang heavy on your hands. You did it for one reason: so that you would have more time for your priorities.

Maybe the book you always wanted to write. Maybe getting home on time to dinner. Making calls to worthy employees who don't get enough of your time. Maybe time to clear your desk between meetings and have 15 minutes to prepare for the next one. Maybe just time to go to lunch most days. Only you know what desires you have been leaving unfulfilled because you couldn't find time for them.

Now you DO have time for them. You are now possessed of an unimaginable luxury – time to fulfill your fondest desires.

You have made others comfortable with your Time Locks... so you would have **more time for your priorities.**

There's a really good reason **most people don't like to plan:** we end up personally accountable for our plan!

But, how do we make certain that this newly recovered time is utilized in the most productive and profitable of ways, leveraged to the fullest and not squandered?

And how will you keep those promises that you made to your Time Bandits about your Time Locking proposals and your responses to their objections?

The answer is my version of the 80/20 Rule. I call it **"The Critical Few versus the Minor Many."**

Focusing on your Critical Few versus your Minor Many is what will maximize your ability to keep and exceed your quid pro quo commitments to your Time Bandits. Remember, you told them that, qualitatively, you would use the time you had been able to create for increased productivity and/or service and quantitatively increasing your results. As a result, they will expect you to demonstrate a related "Step-by-Step Time-Managed Implementation Action Plan" for utilizing the Time Surplus.

Behavioral planning is the pathway for keeping the promises made. In the next chapters I will provide the means and method for the behavioral planning needed, culminating in a bilateral agreement with the Time Bandits that actually formalizes the qualitative and quantitative commitments undertaken.

Additionally, through behavioral planning, we can become organized. We can gain and maintain control over exactly how we allocate our time. However, few people love to plan. We like to conceive, and we like to do, while planning often seems like it spoils the fun of doing. But remember, without a plan, all you have is a wish, and little hope of accomplishing it.

There's a really good reason most people don't like to plan: we end up personally accountable for our plan! Feeling personally accountable is not a cozy feeling; instinctively we'd rather not be held accountable – for anything, for any reason, not to others, not even to ourselves.

A plan also feels like we are sacrificing flexibility. What if a step in the plan doesn't turn out right? What if one of my colleagues in the plan does not act as expected? Good points, but the solution is not, *"Let's skip the plan in favor of flexibility."* The solution is to create, for every action plan, a **contingency plan.**

Even with a contingency plan, I find that many people insist that structured planning is not necessary. They prefer to operate intuitively and emotionally "enslaved to the freedom" of not planning; that way they get to do what they feel like, when they want to, and the way they want to. They might say, *"Things always change. And if they don't, my mood changes. I do just as well playing it by ear."*

If that's truly the way you feel, *may the time management gods be with you!!!*

You see, *"if you don't plan to succeed, you simply plan to fail."* That's a basic truism in just about everything in life as well as in business. Please consider the following given realities:

Would you ever consider building a house without a detailed set of plans?

Would you ever consider **building a house** without a detailed set of plans?

And even if you wanted to, did you think that without a set of plans you could get a financial institution to underwrite the cost of construction, not to mention getting your construction ideas through your local municipal planning board or town engineer? I don't think so.

How about a business? Would you consider even starting a business without a structured business plan? Again, I don't think so. And even if you would, do you think you could get investors to join you? That won't happen.

Let's face it, you and I, without a good set of plans, would be set adrift like a rudderless ship. It's for this reason that I keep stressing the necessity for planning, meticulous planning, at every level, beginning with the audit of your own time and workflow, to the types of interruptions you have each day, to the time wasted versus the time you can gain through Time Locking.

You see, if we don't plan we become susceptible to two laws of human behavior. The first law states that *"No one will manage their time in such a way as to free up enough time to do that which they don't want to do in the first place."*

The second is based on Parkinson's Law, which reminds us that "nature hates vacuums" and, therefore, "work will expand to fill to those vacuums of time." The result is that unless we plan, we will fill the vacuums with what Parkinson calls "busy work."

In behavioral planning, the very first step is to identify our priorities – or what I call the **Critical Few** – versus the **Minor Many** – those other, less important "busy work" tasks to which we can allocate the time that we don't need for our Critical Few.

When we get finished with this chapter, I know you'll agree that *"just playing it by ear"* is not a good alternative to structured, actionable, step-by-step implementation planning.

In fact, what you'll find is that without the concepts behind the Critical Few approach to 80/20 prioritization and planning, you may be treating all tasks with equal importance. I call this phenomenon the **Egalitarian Time-Management Behavior Phenomenon.**

Newsflash: not everything we do is of equal importance, no matter how it feels when our entire to-do list is racing around our brain. For example, if you are a salesperson about to work on your book of accounts, and you are behind goal and have a limited amount of time, then obviously you'll contact your most profitable clients first and work down the list.

Prioritization is the essential process for understanding what should be our highest concern, or, on the other hand, how we deprive ourselves of the calmness that comes only with the confidence that our priorities are well-chosen and provided for with sufficient time.

I first came to understand all of this when, at 33, I persuaded Roy Rogers, the famous movie and television cowboy, to become my business management client. He'd been my idol as a kid growing up in New York, where I had even worked the bull and bronco riding chutes at Madison Square Garden during the Roy Rogers Wild West rodeos. I had dreamed of riding Trigger next to the great Roy Rogers and wondered what it would be like to know such a man. So you can imagine how seriously I took being his manager.

By the time he became my client, Roy had already completed well over a hundred, 30-minute, black-and-white TV shows, each of which had appeared on network TV and syndicated numerous times.

They were pretty worn out and, frankly, so was Roy. He grew weary of the film business. Except for Dale Evans, his wife, forcing him into movies and live theater engagements, Roy (who by this time was suffering from angina) would have preferred to find some way wherein he could generate the same revenues and not work so darn hard.

Because of Roy's international iconic fame and familiarity, fans wanted and would pay for mementos, including anything bearing the name, likeness, and image of the king of the cowboys, Roy Rogers and his television (and real) family including Dale, Nellie Bell (his jeep), Trigger (his horse), and Bullet (his ever faithful German Shepherd dog).

I first came to understand prioritization when, at 33, I persuaded **Roy Rogers,** the famous movie and television cowboy, to become my business management client.

I discovered, much to my surprise, that, in contrast with what we had always assumed, **more than 80% of Roy's revenues** were generated from commercial tie-ups, licensing of his name, and making simple personal appearances.

The use of Roy's name was generating steady revenue, especially so whenever he made personal appearances that required no more of him than autographs and reminiscences. It therefore didn't take much persuasion from me for Roy to recognize that theme-park appearances, in combination with commercial tie-ups, were the way he should spend the majority of his time and energy. He was satisfied with just doing the autograph sessions, but his wife, Dale, was not.

You see, Roy and Dale were philanthropists, and she wanted him to make more films and appear at more rodeos, as well as anything else that would generate revenues for their charities.

Roy confided in me that he would do whatever Dale asked, but he really didn't want to.

Roy trusted me so much that, when for tax reasons he was forced to dissolve his personal holding company and sell off the rights to his films, I made a deal with him to purchase his entire library. As a result, our relationship became that of partners (vs. just client/ manager) in the library's redistribution which resulted in Roy's financial and personal image success.

As his partner, I looked into the numbers a little closer. I discovered, much to my surprise, that, in contrast with what we had always assumed, more than 80% of Roy's revenues were generated from commercial tie-ups, licensing of his name, and making simple personal appearances. Making films and performing in rodeos would take up a lot more of his time and generate less return. The best use of his time, financially speaking, would be to continue the personal appearances and to expand the licensing of his name to such products as Levi Jeans, toy guns, chaps, etc.

Incidentally, prior to Roy, there were only a few (if any) celebrities aggressively implementing commercial tie-ups. Roy and I went on to use his name for the Roy Rogers national restaurant chain and for – the then-largest deal in the history of commercial tie-ups – a 5,000-acre theme park that I negotiated which was to be named "Roy Rogers' Western World" with the hopes of becoming the equivalent of Knott's Berry Farm in Southern California. *(See inset on Pages 176–177.)* Unfortunately, because of his worsening angina and the untimely death of his daughter, the park was never built.

While the movies and rodeos had laid the foundation for Roy's existing revenue, they no longer drove it. Having proved to Dale that Roy had the right priorities, financially speaking, she readily acceded to his time allocation.

My discovery about Roy's revenue distribution was a perfect Illustration of the **Pareto Principle**. In 1906, Vilfredo Pareto, an Italian economist, observed that in his village, 20% of the villagers

VILFREDO PARETO

had 80% of the wealth. He surveyed other townships and found a similar distribution.

Since then, management experts and economists have used the principle to highlight the need for careful, fact-based prioritization in everything from health, safety, and customer profitability to, of course, our own subject here, the allocation of time and resources.

It's a fact of life that applies across the board from business to your personal life. 20% of your clients bring in 80% of your revenues. 80% of your stress is caused by 20% of your problems. In network television, it's the concept of "prime time;" the three hours of prime time produce 80% of the revenues despite being only 20% of the programming.

Look, everybody knows about 80/20, but that doesn't mean everybody knows how to apply it in their time management challenges. As it's commonly stated, *"Everybody knows the Ten Commandments, but we still got sin."* If we were born good at prioritizing, you wouldn't be reading this book and I wouldn't have written it. Besides, applying 80/20 in finance is one thing, in manufacturing it's another, and in time management still another.

In time allocation, the idea is for you to allocate 80% of your time to the 20% of your tasks that deliver the greatest return on your effort. In other words, you shouldn't just "work smart," you should "work smart on the **right things.**"

However, just knowing 80/20 isn't knowing what to prioritize. Often our top priorities – our Critical Few – lurk in the background behind the Minor Many, disguised as important. So, I utilize a technique I call the **Given Reality Test** to differentiate and not treat the 80 like the 20 and vice versa.

With the Given Reality Test, we focus on the effects of a problem and the consequence of not solving the problem. For example, if three critical problems have been identified and management is

ROY ROGERS' WESTERN WORLD

Roy Rogers, left; Ed Brown, center; Pat Boone, seated.

In 1966, the president of Sunnyland Orange Juice in Florida (who was also a client), Bill Canole, explained to me that through the connections he had with Disney, he had learned that Disney was accumulating land in area known as Bay Lakes, which is part of the Orlando/Titusville/Daytona Beach highway triangle.

Orlando Sentinel
'Tis a Privilege to Live in Central Florida
Orlando, Florida, Sunday, November 28, 1965
$10 Million 'Western World' To Go In Near Disney's Tract

Roy Rogers Plans Area Attraction

Roy Rogers Plans Attraction Near 'Disneyland East'

ORLANDO (AP) - Cowboy star Roy Rogers plans a $10 million tourist attraction near Walt Disney's proposed "Disneyland East" in central Florida. The proposed development was disclosed Sunday by Edward G. Brown of Hollywood, Calif., the movie star's business manager and partner in the project.

"We are negotiating for 5,000 acres in Orange County," Brown said. "We intend to construct a complete western city called

'Roy Rogers' Western World.'"

Brown said the development would include shops, hotels, nightclubs, stables, corrals, a dud ranch and a museum - all with a western motif.

The museum, Brown said, will house a large collection of western artifacts owned by Rogers and valued at "several hundreds of thousands of dollars."

Brown said Western World will be complementary to Disney's project 11 miles west of Orlando.

ROY ROGERS ALSO EYES FLORIDA

ORLANDO, ☞ — Cowboy star Roy Rogers plans a $10 million tourist attraction near Walt Disney's proposed "Disneyland East" in Central Florida.

The proposed development was disclosed yesterday by Edward G. Brown, Hollywood, Calif., Rogers' business manager and partner in the project.

"We are negotiating for 5,000 acres in Orange County," Brown said. "We intend to construct a complete western city called 'Roy Rogers' Western World'."

Brown said the development would include shops, hotels, night clubs, stables, corrals, a dude ranch and a museum — all with a western motif.

The museum, Brown said, would house a large collection of western artifacts owned by Rogers and valued at "several hundreds of thousands of dollars."

OUR EDITORS SAY
Wild West In Florida

Roy Rogers, singing cowboy of the movies, says he is shopping for 5,000 acres in the Orlando area on which to build a town, dude ranch, and all the trappings of the American Old West for a tourist attraction.

It would complement, not compete with, the big attraction by Walt Disney. However, Rogers would spend only $10 million, compared with the $100 million Disney says it may take to put his plan together.

The more the merrier, we say. We wish one of these entrepreneurs would discover the charms and potentials of this part of Florida, but we have to recognize that South Central Florida has the location, close to our state's big population centers, as well as the year-around climate, which will keep the turnstiles

clicking when the winter visitors return home.

Besides, a cow country frontier town won't be as incongruous in the area south of Orlando as it would be in other parts of Florida. The rest of the world doesn't know it, but that is cow country as surely as Texas is, and it has an open range heritage as bona fide — if not as storied — as the wild and wooly West.

Roy Rogers and his wife and leading lady, Dale Evans, are known as people of rare good character in Hollywood. Like Disney, they may be depended upon to give Florida an attraction that rises above the shoddiness of the average tourist trap —a place that adds to the growing list of high quality entertainments for our visitors and our residents.

$10000 REWARD

A visitor to Florida could drive from Daytona Beach, where he could enjoy a wonderful climate, extraordinary beaches, and the Daytona race track. Thereafter, continue on to Titusville and observe the preparations for a new rocket launch by NASA. Continuing along the Beeline Highway, a visitor would make his way to Orlando where eventually he would come upon Bay Lakes, the key location for the construction and development of Disney World.

Upon learning of this, Roy Rogers, Pat Boone, and I began to speculate about real estate investment possibilities along the Triangle.

With Roy's immense popularity and because of the commercial value of building a theme park that would complement Disney World in the same way that Knott's Berry Farm complements Disneyland in California, Roy, Pat, and I were offered 5,000 acres for free as long as we selected the site on the Beeline Highway.

Roy Rogers' Western World had accumulated over a dozen commitments from concessionaires such as Sinclair Oil, Winchester, Suzuki, and Carnation, that would have paid for the entire construction of the theme park.

At the time, it was the largest deal in the history of commercial tie-ups. Regrettably, because of the untimely death of Roy's daughter, the theme park was never built.

But how do you know if someone else's urgent is **your** urgent? Just like a smart phone, I have an "app" for that, which I call the **Importance vs. Urgency Prioritization Grid.**

unsure which problem is the most critical, and which must be addressed first, the **effects** of all the problems should be analyzed and compared so that – based on the data – one can choose the problem in need of the immediate attention and resources that will provide the greatest benefit to the organization.

We must also analyze the effect of *not* solving a problem. For example, if the problem is that your personnel are not skilled at selling and you don't solve it with training, you may very well go out of business.

So what happens when someone tells you that solving a problem is urgent to your welfare and/or the welfare of your firm? How do you know if someone else's urgent is your urgent?

Just like a smart phone, I have an "app" for that, which I call the **Importance vs. Urgency Prioritization Grid.** It works by differentiating what's important to us from what's urgent to others. It lets us take situational control by not confusing the two.

Across the grid's X axis we plot **Importance**, by which I mean OUR perspective. What is important to ME and the goals I have committed to?

Along the Y axis I plot Urgency, based on OTHERS' perspectives. I interpret things that are important to others as being urgent. Others include your managers, team members, clients, colleagues — anyone who is putting tasks on your to-do list. When something is urgent to others and important to us as well, then it's a Critical Few.

CF = Critical Few
MM = Minor Many
N = Negotiable

Importance vs. Urgency Prioritization Grid			**Importance (Us)**	
			1. EXTREME	**2.** SOMEWHAT
Urgency (Them)	**A.** EXTREME		CF (CRITICAL FEW)	N (NEGOTIABLE)
	B. SOMEWHAT		N (NEGOTIABLE)	MM (MINOR MANY)

Very often, my wife will say, *"Someone's on the phone, and he says it's urgent."* Then she'll put her hand over the phone and remind me, *"It may be their urgent, not your urgent."*

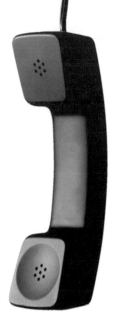

In other words, be skeptical about the urgency, and 90% of the time, she's right. Just as Tommy Wants-to-Please has, you too have so many clients and colleagues who all need/want something from you. You respect them and their desires, but you also have other things to do. You have to learn to prioritize and to admit to yourself what you probably already know: what's urgent – you cannot live without; what's important – you have to deal with but not at the expense of what's urgent.

Let's analyze this difference in terms of what you encounter each day. Think of your five best clients. Go back in time and recall situations when they told you that they needed to talk to you, see you, hear from you because it was "urgent," in their words, but you found that it wasn't. It may have been urgent to them, but it wasn't urgent to you; and had you not reacted, by either taking their call, having the meeting, immediately responding to an email, it wouldn't have made any difference to your relationship or to the welfare of the client.

This is you training yourself to take situational control over your time based on knowing when something isn't really urgent. And in fact, you can negotiate with your client, even your family or boss, to contact them at a time or work with them at a time that's more convenient to you, and do exactly what they want.

So here's the rule:

> If it's urgent to you and it's urgent to them then, as I said, it's a Critical Few and goes in Box A1. If it is somewhat important to them and somewhat important to you, then it's a Minor Many and belongs in Box B2.

My wife will say, *"Someone's on the phone, and he says it's urgent."* Then she'll put her hand over the phone and remind me, *"It may be their urgent, not your urgent."*

Think of Critical Few as those tasks that if they were not completed on time could affect your business, or your ability to stay employed, or the health of a loved one.

Once your Critical Few are completed then the items in Box A2 and B1 are to be addressed next depending on their deadlines. These items can become Critical Few as time marches on and their deadlines approach.

A copy of the grid is in the appendix for your use in analyzing and differentiating your Critical Few from your Minor Many tasks, roles, and responsibilities.

Think of Critical Few as those tasks that if they were not completed on time could affect your business, or your ability to stay employed, or the health of a loved one.

Think of the Minor Many as those things that could be postponed or completed once a week or month. Think of how you clean your house. We always keep a tidy house, but you don't need a full spring cleaning more than once every few months. However, if you are throwing a party, then doing a full cleaning becomes more critical.

Using the Time-Management Worksheet on the next page, (and also in the appendix) list all of your own real-world tasks and designate them as either Critical Few or Minor Many, keeping in mind the Importance vs. Urgency Prioritization Grid and the 80/20 Rule. Then, indicate whether you perform each task daily, weekly, or monthly.

Now that we have begun to organize our formal structured time management plan through prioritization, we're on our way toward leveraging the time we recaptured to enable us to implement all of our critical initiatives while keeping all the commitments we have made to the Time Bandits.

TIME-MANAGEMENT WORKSHEET

TASK	CF/ MM	FREQ	BATCH	H/E	DOW	TIME LOCK	TIME NEEDED	WHO

For people, **Batch Processing** means saving up repetitive or homogeneous tasks and doing them all at once so that you can gain efficiency and momentum. Fingers go faster, muscle memory happens, distractions disappear.

Batch Processing Planning

Now that you've learned how to identify your Critical Few from your Minor Many so that you can allocate the right amount of time to them, you will quickly find that there still remains a significant time management issue. It is this: everybody has tasks that are somewhat repetitive. They don't require a lot of thinking, but they do take time, usually more time than they should. For me it's checking my emails. For you it might be approving expense reports. Or completing forms. Or scheduling meetings. So I asked myself, is there a way to do them more efficiently?

There is. It's called **Batch Processing.** It's a computer term from the earliest days of computers when punch cards were still used. A bunch of those keypunched cards would be assembled and then run in a batch.

The value of Batch Processing is the momentum that is generated. Computers gain speed when they repeat the same set of tasks over and over. Their pointers get set to the appropriate parts of their memories. For people, Batch Processing means saving up repetitive or homogeneous tasks and doing them all at once so that you can gain efficiency and momentum. Fingers go faster, muscle memory happens, distractions disappear.

You might know someone who can multi-task effortlessly. Most of us however find that when we do, we lose momentum, lose track of what we are doing, and eventually let some things fall through the cracks.

 **Buddy Hackett** was a great comedian whose shtick was to start one joke and then interrupt himself (and drive the audience crazy) by starting another in the middle of the first, and then another in the middle of the second. He could keep five different jokes up and running, riffing back and forth among them, taking the audience wherever he went and back again, and never lose the thread and/or the punch line on any of them, and reap a standing ovation.

It was virtuoso stuff **and** it was the opposite of Batch Processing. It was multi-tasking of the highest order, far more complex than what sometimes passes for multi-tasking today: texting while watching a soccer game, or letting the cat out while leading a conference call. Most human brains can't, as Buddy's could, concentrate on so many different paths without losing the thread, momentum, or energy.

If Buddy is the anti-model for Batch Processing, the model was a commercial artist, well known in cruise ship circles for his paintings of clowns. I visited his studio one day and was surprised to see 35 canvases, all with partially painted clown faces. He saw my surprise and explained, *"Ed, I batch paint. I can paint a chin, another chin, and another chin and do them faster and more accurately than I could do a chin, a nose, and a forehead, and so on. I'm better at my job when I do it this way."*

This painter knew exactly what he was doing. He wasn't striving for another "Mona Lisa" or "Girl with a Pearl Earring." He was striving for dozens of appealing paintings of clowns in various poses. He adapted his work process for his intended results.

*"Ed, I batch paint. I can paint a chin, another chin, and another chin and do them faster and more accurately than I could do a chin, a nose, and a forehead, and so on. **I'm better at my job when I do it this way.**"*

For him, one clown's nose was similar enough to the next clown's nose that painting them drew on a specific skill. By doing 35 noses in a row, he was able to draw on that specific skill, dispose of 35 noses expeditiously, and move on to 35 mouths. He saved himself time and energy, AND – let me stress this last point, he painted better noses and mouths.

When you Batch Process repetitive tasks and set aside the appropriate time for doing them, your quality and your efficiency will improve, and you will enjoy greater focus, momentum, and concentration. In addition, because you will group your tasks ahead of time, you will be spared the nuisance and distraction of those tasks presenting themselves at different times of the day.

If your job is like mine in any respect – if you are ultimately responsible for a group's or a company's ideas, leadership, performance, financials, and so on – then you know that you absolutely have to subtract yourself from day-to-day activity and focus on one pressing matter or another. You have to Time Lock for certain work. In my case, my Time Locks are frequently for the purpose of developing programs, which consists of many different types of tasks: research, writing, debriefing, debugging, testing, and so on.

Over the years, I've gotten better at Time Locking because I learned how to incorporate Batch Processing. I've learned how, even during the creative process of program development, to find homogeneous activities – those that look and feel alike, or require similar skills, or a similar environment. If research for the program calls for five phone calls, then I batch those calls, rather than making one when the need comes up, then going back to writing, and then interrupting myself to make another. If I need to test workshops of a program on my team, I don't assemble them each time I encounter an exercise; I batch the testing to make it efficient all around.

I can assure you, I feel the payoff as I'm doing it. I get better and better at the tasks in each batch precisely **because** I've batched them – because I'm doing them over and over. Like an athlete perfecting a motion until he develops muscle memory – or a painter painting clown noses – I'm perfecting Time Lock performance by incorporating Batch Processing.

If research calls for five phone calls, then **I batch those calls,** rather than making one when the need comes up, then going back to writing, and then interrupting myself to make another.

CRITICAL FEW
A.M.

MINOR MANY
P.M.

It's a good bet that some of your Minor Many tasks do not have daily or even weekly mandatory deadlines. That means **they can be gathered together in a bunch and Batch Processed.**

My wife, who as I said before is a structural engineer, tells me that architects or structural engineers who have more than one project at a time to design, gain momentum by Batch Processing all the columns while their minds are on the column design formula for all the projects. Then they consider the beams, slabs, and so on.

If you do the same, you will experience the thrill of momentum, like a cyclist who gets up so much speed that he can make it up a steep hill without exertion.

Remember my Aunt Letty? When she Focal Locked on her typing assignments with her Smith Corona typewriter, she went into her trance-like state by doing one thing: typing. She didn't type one page and then answer the phone and then type another page. Momentum was her friend, and she knew it.

The point is that by Batch Processing we increase our ability to focus on the task at hand and Focal Lock because we do not disturb ourselves with the need to multi-task.

Now think back to the Minor Many tasks you identified earlier, and consider the deadlines that accompany them. It's a good bet that some, possibly many of them, do not have daily or even weekly mandatory deadlines. That means they can be gathered together in a bunch and Batch Processed.

But let's be clear – even though we might look first among our Minor Many tasks for those that can be Batch Processed, critical tasks can fall into that category, too. The key is, are they repetitive or homogeneous, and can you gain momentum if you perform them as a batch? Even if I'm doing something as high-intensity as observing and coaching executives as part of a training program, I know that I will gain momentum, energy, and skill if I conduct these coaching sessions consecutively, instead of sprinkling other to do's between them.

Remember, **the best tasks to Batch Process** are those tasks that are homogeneous, and are typically repetitive.

If you find yourself constantly shifting gears as you go through your day – bouncing between doing your budget, taking phone calls, answering emails, and meeting with team members, your day holds huge Batch Processing potential. Set aside 30 minutes to answer easy emails. If there's a tough one in there, perhaps a sensitive response to a customer, set aside a different 30 minutes to Time Lock on it. Find what's homogeneous and batch them up for better time management.

So now go back to the Time-Management Worksheet on Page 181 that you used for determining your Critical Few versus your Minor Many, and group as many of the latter as you can for Batch Processing on a daily, weekly, and even monthly basis during your uninterrupted, planned Time Locks. Remember, the best tasks to Batch Process are those tasks that are homogeneous, and are typically repetitive like administrative, operations, and compliance tasks, particularly if they consist of inputting calculations, or callbacks, sales calls, reading and responding to emails, and believe it or not, even coaching, observation, and observational feedback. Enter Y for "Yes" if it can be batched, or N for "No" if it can't be batched, next to the task.

Now that you've learned how to carve out work that can be Batch Processed, the next step is to determine when to tackle your various tasks. In the next chapter, we'll help you categorize your "Hard vs. Easy" work, and choose the right time for each.

Planning for Hard vs. Easy

Not all work is created equal. Some is harder for you, some is easier. Nor are all hours of the day or week equal. You have more energy during some than you do during others. It only makes good time-management sense to align your hard work with your high-energy times, and your easy tasks with your periods of low energy.

The New York Times recently wrote about three men doing time in prison who appeared before the parole board. Each had completed at least two-thirds of his sentence, but only one was granted parole.

- In one case, heard at 8:50 a.m., the man was serving a 30-month sentence for fraud.
- In another, heard at 3:10 p.m., the man was serving a 16-month sentence for assault.
- In the third, heard at 4:25 p.m., the man was serving a 30-month sentence for fraud.

Parole denied.

Prisoners who appeared before the judge in the morning received parole about 70 percent of the time, while **those who appeared late in the day** were paroled less than 10 percent of the time.

187

Decision fatigue helps explain why ordinarily sensible people get angry at colleagues. No matter how rational and high-minded you try to be, **you can't make decision after decision without paying a biological price.**

The *Times* article states:

"There was a pattern to the parole board's decisions, but it wasn't related to the men's ethnic backgrounds, crimes, or sentences. It was all about timing, as researchers discovered by analyzing more than 1,100 decisions over the course of a year. Judges, who would hear the prisoners' appeals and then get advice from the other members of the board, approved parole in about a third of the cases, but the probability of being paroled fluctuated wildly throughout the day. Prisoners who appeared early in the morning received parole about 70 percent of the time, while those who appeared late in the day were paroled less than 10 percent of the time.

"The odds favored the prisoner who appeared at 8:50 a.m. — and he did in fact receive parole."

The others, the article continued, *"were just asking for parole at the wrong time of day. There was nothing malicious or even unusual about the judges' behavior… The mental work of ruling on case after case, whatever the individual merits, wore them down. This sort of decision fatigue can make quarterbacks prone to dubious choices late in the game and C.F.O.'s prone to disastrous dalliances late in the evening. It routinely warps the judgment of everyone, executive and nonexecutive, rich and poor — in fact, it can take a special toll on the poor. Yet few people are even aware of it, and researchers are only beginning to understand why it happens and how to counteract it.*

"Decision fatigue helps explain why ordinarily sensible people get angry at colleagues and families, splurge on clothes, buy junk food at the supermarket and can't resist the dealer's offer to rustproof their new car. No matter how rational and high-minded you try to be, you can't make decision after decision without paying a biological price. It's different from ordinary physical fatigue — you're not consciously aware of being tired — but you're low on mental energy.

"The more choices you make throughout the day, the harder each one becomes for your brain, and eventually it looks for shortcuts, usually in either of two very different ways. One shortcut is to become reckless: to act impulsively instead of expending the energy to first think through the consequences. (Sure, tweet that photo! What could go wrong?)

"The other shortcut is the ultimate energy saver: do nothing. Instead of agonizing over decisions, avoid any choice. Ducking a decision often creates bigger problems in the long run, but for the moment, it eases the mental strain. You start to resist any change, any potentially risky move — like releasing a prisoner who might commit a crime. **So the fatigued judge on a parole board takes the easy way out, and the prisoner keeps doing time."***

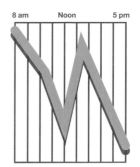

Your capabilities change over the course of the work day, so that **you should align your tasks** with your energy peaks and valleys.

If you're like me, you find some of your work to be hard, and some to be relatively easy. I don't mean hard in the Sisyphean sense, or that you find it disagreeable. I mean hard in that it requires serious concentration from you, and doing it depletes you of significant energy. Conversely, you have some tasks that are easy in the sense that you can toss them off without difficulty, losing little energy in the process.

What does all that have to do with time management? It says that your capabilities change over the course of the work day, so that you should align your tasks with your energy peaks and valleys. Yours may not be like mine or your colleagues', but you have them; and whether you are fully aware of it or not, your performance is affected by them.

I'm intimately familiar with my own energy cycles. I love writing new training programs, but when I do they consume tremendous focus and energy. On the other hand, holding team meetings is a breeze for me. Notice I'm not saying it's less important – just that it doesn't deplete my energy.

I am also a morning person, which means my energy is at its highest when the day begins. So I would be foolish to hold my team meetings in the morning and wait until the waning hours of

* Tierney, John. "Do You Suffer From Decision Fatigue?" New York Times. www.nytimes.com/2011/08/21/magazine/do-you-suffer-from-decision-fatigue.html

You want to use your **peak** parts of the day for your Critical Few, and your **valleys** for your Minor Many.

the day to write new programs. I take my Time Locks – my alone time, doing my most concentrated thinking and creating and my hardest, most analytical work – when I'm infused with morning optimism and energy.

I try to be attentive to the energy cycles of my colleagues, too. Late in the day is typically not a good time to call on one of our salespeople and try to get him to brainstorm his approach on a major account. Early morning is not a good time to interrupt the writer I work with.

Are you familiar with your own energy cycles? For optimum time management, you should be. Earlier we said that your work consists of what we call your Critical Few tasks and the Minor Many. Often the Critical Few are the most challenging – the hardest – while the Minor Many are easier. If so, you want to use your peak parts of the day for your Critical Few, and your valleys for your Minor Many. By doing so, you make the best use of the time that you recaptured by Time Locking and Focal Locking.

Instead of doing things "as they come up," or in some other indeterminate pattern, correctly aligning certain kinds of tasks with certain times of the day or week lets you concentrate more assiduously, perform more effectively, and, in turn, produce fewer mistakes. Since mistakes waste time, doing things the right way the first time is an underappreciated time saver.

That means laying out an explicit plan: choose a specific time and day to work on your Critical Few; set aside other periods for your Minor Many.

One common mistake is to automatically start out the day working on the easy things. Sometimes it's a well-intentioned mistake: *"If I get these nuisances out of the way, then I can be completely focused on my hard work."* Other times it's more pragmatic: *"Let me get into the swing of things by tackling these minor items – that will give me the energy and incentive for my important work."*

Rarely does that work. "Little" things often take longer than they should, and they deplete the fresh energy of the morning that is best reserved for hard jobs. Higher energy doesn't just mean more strength, it also means more clarity.

This is a good place to raise a warning flag about what I call **"Energy Vampires."** I've never spoken that phrase to a training class without seeing rueful smiles appear immediately. You know exactly what an energy vampire is, and you can name yours without a moment's reflection, can't you?

Energy vampires come in different packages. Most have a negative bent, incessantly warning you that your hard work won't be appreciated, or complaining about the deadline, the tools, the pay, or the client, or citing only obstacles, never pathways. I get weary writing about them. Some disguise their energy-sucking ways with a cheerful exterior masking a political agenda

Energy vampires come in different packages. Most have a negative bent, incessantly warning you that your hard work won't be appreciated, or complaining about the deadline, the tools, the pay, or the client, or citing only obstacles, never pathways.

that takes your focus off your real work and leaves you fretting about things you can't control.

You can't hope to get through life without associating with energy vampires, but know who yours are. Mentally label them so. If you can't change them, avoid them. If you can't avoid them, short circuit them – plan ways to limit how long their fangs remain in you. And after they leave you, use the "counterpunching" technique to restore your own energy, optimism, and good humor.

Certainly there will be exceptions on an individual basis, but generally work that's difficult and challenging should be done first thing Monday morning. Then do the next hardest thing Tuesday morning, easier things at the end of the day, and the easiest things at the end of the week. Monday, Tuesday, and Wednesday mornings are prime time for most people.

I use Friday to plan for Monday, sometimes the whole week, so that on Monday, I can hit the ground running. Again, your energy cycles may be different, but the point is that not every day of the week, and not every hour of the day, should be treated equally.

Different cultures would, of course, alter this schedule, but all with the same goal in mind of using high-energy periods for important work. As a newly hired salesman in Spain told us, *"It wears me out to watch you Americans try to get so much work done right after lunch. Why not take the time off for a siesta or pure enjoyment, and come back refreshed for hard work later in the day?"*

A banker from Ireland once told me that he thought I was crazy for suggesting that he have focused sales meetings on Monday mornings. He said, *"Monday mornings are only good for sobering up from the weekend. We don't do anything difficult until Tuesday."*

Regardless, the point is to match your work to your energy for top performance.

Now, see how aligning your work with your peaks and valleys creates a wise schedule for you. Using the same **Time-Management Worksheet** you've been developing for the Critical Few versus the Minor Many and Batch Processing, evaluate whether each task is hard or easy. Then, enter H for "Hard" or E for "Easy" in the column next to the task. Once you have your tasks designated as H or E, even before you do anything more with your planning sheet, you will be able to see at a glance which tasks will come early and which ones will come later.

Generally **work that's difficult and challenging** should be done first thing Monday morning.

The Planning Protocol

What do you call it when, before every single pitch, the pitcher tugs his hat brim, paws the ground, claps ball to glove, straightens his shoulders, takes a deep breath? Or when, before every serve, the tennis player inspects the balls, discards the worn ones, bounces the chosen one precisely four times, stares across the net, bites his lip, and bends to serve?

Habits? Tendencies? True, but more than that, they are protocols. They are routines that focus the athlete, block out any external distractions, and set the course for a perfect delivery that looks exactly like the one they practiced for thousands of hours. Even with the bases loaded, or at match point at Wimbledon, if the athlete follows his protocol, his body will perform as trained, not throw a wild pitch or double fault.

Protocols are routines that focus the athlete, block out any external distractions, and set the course for a perfect delivery that looks exactly like the one they practiced for thousands of hours.

193

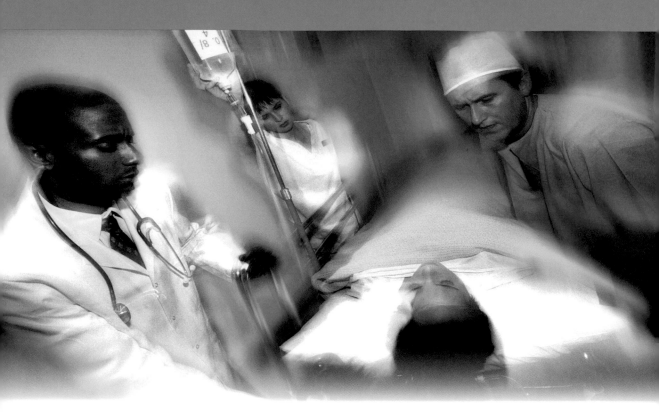

During every medical emergency, ER physicians and all others on duty will religiously employ **the same protocol over and over.**

A doctor friend of mine likes to describe protocols in the medical arena. He told me about what he went through as a young physician, just out of medical school, beginning his career working in a medical emergency room, trying to convert chaos into an orderly environment.

The protocols the ER employed were a code of conduct – the rules, if you will – to follow rigorously in a given situation. These protocols have been tested and proven and practiced to lead to the best outcomes for any given situation.

During every medical emergency, ER physicians and all others on duty will religiously employ the same protocol over and over. All parties involved know the exact steps that will be taken and in which order for every kind of medical emergency that arrives in their midst. The protocol ensures that when physicians gather around a gasping patient, they know without having to ask whether the patient's airways have been checked, if coughing has been encouraged, if the Heimlich maneuver has been employed, if an injection has been made, if certain equipment is being brought to the room.

They know all this without pausing or asking because these steps have been prescribed and practiced. As a result, they can be confident they are making the best use of equipment, education, and protocols in order to greatly increase the prospect of a favorable outcome for the patient.

I realized that doing things the same way every time wasn't just great for super-technical, life and death situations. On the contrary, protocols – tested, proven, predictable behaviors for favorable outcomes – can be employed to solve other pressing problems, especially those where cause and effect are uncertain and the wrong assessment could create more problems than it solves.

So we began to use protocols for helping our clients solve such problems. Kaiser Steel asked us to resolve a puzzling manufacturing problem in the manufacturing unit where they produced tin-coated steel for tin cans.

It was a quality control problem. Only 62% of their output met acceptable quality levels. This was significantly unprofitable as they had to run production lines twice to produce what should have been achieved in a single run.

In our discussions, they told us that they would be thrilled if they could go from 62% to 85% quality production on a regular basis. It was 1980, so we came up with a campaign called "85 in 80."

Within about six months, they did not merely hit 85 in 80. They were consistently averaging 92% quality by the end of 1980, a level they previously thought impossible.

What brought this remarkable success was the **DERSSIM Logic System,** which derived its name from the following protocol:

> **Protocols can be employed to solve other pressing problems,** especially those where cause and effect are uncertain and the wrong assessment could create more problems than it solves.

DERSSIM

- ✔ **D**efine the problem.
- ✔ Clarify the **E**ffects.
- ✔ Identify the **R**easons.
- ✔ Identify **S**olutions.
- ✔ Create and utilize a **S**olution **I**mplementation **M**ethodology.

The **"cart"** is the numerical goal while the **"horse"** is the behavioral goal. You must set your behavioral goals concurrently with your numerical goals. Moreover, you must set deadlines for them, because all goals, behavioral or numerical, without deadlines are worthless.

By carefully following that specific DERSSIM protocol, Kaiser was able to single out the problem to be addressed, articulate the effects they wished to eradicate, isolate the reasons for the problem from all possible reasons considered, propose effective solutions, and then (and only then) create the methodology for implementing the solutions. Each step performed in precise order, each step proceeding only from the previous step.

The lesson for me from this success was this: all planning, whether it's for time management or creating a company's vision, must be accompanied by a protocol – known and practiced routinely.

So to leverage the time you have now learned to create – to use it with maximum efficiency, you need a **Planning Protocol,** and here it is: I refer to it as the **What, How, Who, How Many, and By When Protocol.**

Wait!! Don't even think about applying this protocol without first determining the goals of your plan. Bear in mind you have two kinds: one is behavioral (what you will do), and one is numerical (what you will achieve).

To distinguish between them, think of the horse and cart metaphor. In this metaphor the "cart" is the numerical goal while the "horse" is the behavioral goal. Since I know you would never consider putting the cart before the horse, you must set your behavioral goals concurrently with your numerical goals. Moreover, you must set deadlines for them, because all goals, behavioral or numerical, without deadlines are worthless.

Here's how the What, How, Who, How Many, and By When?
Protocol works:

- **What** means what is the task that you're planning to achieve?

- **How** means how will you achieve those tasks?

- **Who** means, other than yourself, who else will you be relying on to achieve these tasks?

- **How Many** means how many of these tasks must be implemented to achieve your goals?

- **By When** means by when are you planning to get started with your task, and by when will you be finished?

If you have carefully fleshed out and implemented this protocol, you absolutely will be on the road to an effective and achievable time-managed step-by-step implementation action plan.

Remember, just like the emergency room personnel, you are meticulously following a specific protocol – one that has been tested, proven, and practiced – so that when you find yourself in the hubbub of the work day, you have increased your chances of positive outcomes.

With that basic understanding, please go back to the Time-Management Worksheet that we have been filling out in the previous chapters and complete the "Time Needed" and "Who" columns. By utilizing the worksheet, we have, in fact, been applying the protocol all along.

In this next chapter, we will use the completed form to create your own customized Structured Time-Managed Workflow Implementation Action Plan.

Remember, **you are following a specific protocol** so that when you find yourself in the hubbub of the work day, you have increased your chances of positive outcomes.

CHAPTER

11:30

You now have all the information and knowledge you need to successfully **recapture your time.** That's a remarkable milestone.

The Implementation Action Plan

Remember Tommy Wants-to-Please back in Chapter 3:00? If you winced when you read about his desperate day, I understand – I winced when I wrote about it. You might have thought, *"Get a plan, man!"* But you know, Tommy **had** a plan, or thought he did. He knew exactly what his priority was that day, and he kept trying and trying – and failing and failing.

But what he thought was a plan was actually an intention. A good intention, but it was only What – what he intended to do. Not How, with Whom, How Many, By When – none of the particulars that convert a good intention into a workable plan with near certainty of success.

At this point, you have all the information and knowledge you need to successfully **recapture your time.** That's a remarkable milestone. Congratulations. That's the result you wanted, isn't it? You wanted to put an end to being frustrated by the interruptions that steal your time, and to be master or mistress of your own time, finding time to do what matters.

Just one thing remains. You've heard it before: *"Successful people don't plan results, they plan actions."*

Planning results? That's just fantasizing: *"My plan to get my finances in order is to be a lottery winner."*

But planning actions? That's reaching out for the future you want and bringing it back to the present where you can do something about it.

Planning is asking yourself, *"What are the concrete steps that I can take today, starting*

*right this minute, in fact, so that step after step leads inevitably to the result I intend? Now that I know **how** to prevent interruptions and use my time wisely, how do I turn that knowledge into action?"*

That's the purpose of this chapter. I don't want to get you this close to success but leave you just short of it.

Everything covered up to now needs to become manifested in your customized **Structured Time-Managed Workflow Implementation Action Plan.** First, however, let's sum up the key basics I've covered up to now.

Now that you know how to prevent interruptions, how do you **turn that knowledge into action?**

1. Remember that behavioral goals, without deadlines, are simply worthless.

2. For simplicity and clarity purposes, use the planning protocol.
   - What?
   - How?
   - Who?
   - How Many?
   - By When?

3. When using the protocol, remember to apply the 80/20 Rule and that the rule means separating your Critical Few from your Minor Many.

4. Unlike the Minor Many, your Critical Few are non-negotiable and must be given the highest priority.

5. When defining the Critical Few versus the Minor Many apply the **Given Reality Test** and the **Importance vs. Urgency Prioritization Grid.**

6. Always remember that when it comes to Time Locking and Batch Processing, if you don't Focal Lock then it will not work.

7. Do what's hard when you have most of your energy, and do what's easy when you have the least.

8. Don't go into planning blindly. Visualize yourself as a *TBS* athlete preparing for a major competition on game day. Only, in this case, you'll be competing against the inertia and the centrifugal force of your real life, where, who knows, you're bound to run into a Time Bandit or two.

Imagine now that Tommy, having read *TBS,* has **taken total control of his time** and now is in control of his life.

At this point, after having examined and practiced the methods to manage your time and workflow, think about Tommy Wants-to-Please, who fell on his sword trying to find the time and energy to please everybody, only to find himself in the AIAI-EKG Hospital of Aggravation, Irritation, Anger, and Impatience.

Imagine now that Tommy, having read *TBS,* has taken total control of his time and now is in control of his life. He has mastered Time Locking and negotiated Time Locking agreements with everyone at work and in his life. He has recovered over 50% of his time and has leveraged it by Batch Processing and utilizing prioritization and the planning protocol. Having mastered all of these techniques, Tommy has completed his time-managed step-by-step implementation action plan. His plan now looks like this:

Hour/Day	Monday	Tuesday	Wednesday	Thursday	Friday
8:00 a.m.	Respond to urgent customer/colleague inquiries Check e-mail				
8:30 a.m.	Conduct Critical Few Hot Topic team mtg	Check e-mail	Check e-mail	Check e-mail	Check e-mail
		Daily Briefing	Daily Briefing & 48-Hour Follow-Up	Daily Briefing	Daily Briefing
9:00 a.m.	Record commitments	Implement team mtg focus	Implement team mtg focus	Implement team mtg focus	Proactive Outbound Calls
9:30 a.m.	Review e-mail & call backs	Prep for Observations	AOC	Prep for Observations	AOC
10:00 a.m.	Implement team mtg focus	Observe Project Mgr conduct customer Needs Analysis	One-on-One Coaching	Observe Project Mgr conduct customer Needs Analysis	One-on-One Coaching
10:30 a.m.					
11:00 a.m.			Proactive Outbound Calls		AOC
11:30 a.m.		AOC		AOC	
12:00 p.m.	Lunch	Lunch	Lunch	Lunch	Lunch
1:00 p.m.	Proactive Outbound Calls	Proactive Outbound Calls	Proactive Outbound Calls	Prep for Skill Building	Proactive Outbound Calls
1:30 p.m.				Skill Building with Max	
2:00 p.m.		Prep for Skill Building			
2:30 p.m.		Skill Building with Jamie	Return non-critical calls & e-mails	Prep for Skill Building	
3:00 p.m.				Skill Building with Marcia	Return non-critical calls & e-mails
3:30 p.m.	Return non-critical calls & e-mails	Return non-critical calls & e-mails			
4:00 p.m.			AOC	Proactive Outbound Calls	Gather week's results
4:30 p.m.		AOC	Debrief with Mgr	AOC/return calls	
5:00 p.m.	Daily Debriefing	Daily Debriefing	Daily Debriefing	Daily Debriefing	End-of-Week Debriefing
5:30 p.m.	Planning	Planning	Planning	Planning	Attend Mgr's End-of-Week Debriefing
6:00 p.m.					Planning

As you can see, since Tommy read *TBS* he has gained the confidence to take control of his life at work. In order to ensure Time Locking and Batch Processing would work, Tommy successfully negotiated arrangements with his colleagues for a Mutual Time Lock Agreement, enabling each of them to avoid interruptions while Batch Processing. Friday rolled around and Tommy planned for the following week.

Let's look in on Tommy's entire Monday. Since it was Tommy's intention to do the more challenging tasks in the morning and the easier tasks in the afternoon, Tommy elected to Time Lock on Monday at 8:30 am to conduct an uninterrupted, "Critical Few Hot Topic Team Meeting" with his direct reports.

At 9:15, Tommy opened his Time Lock, collected and reviewed his emails and made a list of all his callbacks. Since none of the callback requests appeared to be urgent, and since they would be relatively easy to make, Tommy elected to wait until 3:00 that afternoon to return the calls. Having had a spectacular Time Locked, Focal Locked, and Batch Processed morning and having completed all of his more difficult tasks, it was now time for Tommy to have a well-deserved lunch.

After lunch, Tommy used the hours of 1:00 to 3:00 p.m. to proactively contact the clients whose needs required his undivided attention. At 3:00, Tommy's energy had begun to run down. Tommy devoted the remaining two hours to complete

Tommy was even on time for dinner with his family, something he had been unable to do when he was trying to please everybody, reacting to every unwanted interruption, and having no control over his time and workflow.

relatively Minor Many tasks such as returning the calls and emails he had received earlier. Since the balance of Tommy's week will incorporate team meeting follow-up actions, Tommy has already planned when, and under what circumstances, he will include coaching, observation, and feedback.

As Tommy left the office, he felt a great deal of job satisfaction since he got his Monday off to a great start and was looking forward to Tuesday, as well as the rest of the week feeling organized, prepared, and optimistic; and he was even on time for dinner with his family, something he had been unable to do when he was trying to please everybody, reacting to every unwanted interruption, and having no control over his time and workflow.

Using the Time-Management Worksheet that you've been completing in the previous chapters as the source for transferring your weekly tasks, please do as Tommy did and create your own daily, weekly, and even monthly, time-managed action plans on the following schedule.

You are almost finished with this exercise, but two critical parts remain. First, look over the plan you have just created. After you filled in your calendar with all the activities you plan to do – your Time Locks, your Batch Processing, your hard, your easy, your Critical Few, and your Minor Many, how does your week look? Is it as jam-packed as it would have been before?

I'm going to surmise that you discovered a few gaps. Purely as a result of structuring your week deliberately, you have freed up time that is as yet unallocated.

HOUR/DAY	MON	TUE	WED	THU	FRI
8:00 a.m.					
8:30 a.m.					
9:00 a.m.					
9:30 a.m.					
10:00 a.m.					
10:30 a.m.					
11:00 a.m.					
11:30 a.m.					
Noon					
12:30 p.m.					
1:00 p.m.					
1:30 p.m.					
2:00 p.m.					
2:30 p.m.					
3:00 p.m.					
3:30 p.m.					
4:00 p.m.					
4:30 p.m.					
5:00 p.m.					
5:30 p.m.					
6:00 p.m.					
6:30 p.m.					
7:00 p.m.					
7:30 p.m.					

When you are satisfied with your action plan, one important step still remains: **sharing it.**

So now you should take another good look at your week and see if you have given your Critical Few enough time, or if you could dedicate some of that recaptured time to perhaps a longer Time Lock for a particularly important or challenging project. You may want to save that time if you know the week ahead could be filled with surprises for some reason – a new product roll-out, or a system changeover.

The point is, don't just leave precious time to be consumed indiscriminately. Socrates said, *"The unexamined life is not worth living."* I say, *"The unexamined action plan is not worth working."*

Then, when you are satisfied with your action plan, at least to the extent you can logically plan your week, one important step still remains: **sharing it.**

You share it with **your manager** so that he or she can validate your priorities – or be prompted to advise you to change them for some reason. Be ready to be flexible on that and to adapt your plan.

You share it with **your colleagues** so that you can count on them to cover for you during your Time Locks, and so that they know when you can reciprocate. You don't want to be surprised next Tuesday when you have to abandon your Time Lock because your backup is off that day.

If you're a manager, you share it with **your people.** Your action plan is a perfect window on your priorities, and they will adapt theirs accordingly.

Now that you have completed this exercise, you should find yourself with a planning document that gives you confidence that, if you follow it well, you will create even more time for yourself and improve business outcomes for your company. In the next chapter, we will show you how you can instill that same confidence in your colleagues and your bosses.

Mutual Charter Agreement

12:00

The Time Bandit Solution can finally eliminate all of the chaos and all of the suffering that you've had to endure due to interruptions and all of the related Time-Loss Factors.

But, as the poet John Donne wrote, *"No man is an island."* You haven't solved the problem of time slipping away until you've gained the cooperation of your colleagues, bosses, their bosses, and so on. You still have to convince them that what's good for you is also good for them. But what if they, unlike you, have not read *The Time Bandit Solution*? They will not easily understand the benefits of your new way of managing your time. And, for this reason, they may not easily understand how and why they would benefit. That leaves you with the obligation of explaining it. Because you have mastered the secret, you will want to share it.

Because you have mastered the secret, **you will want to share it.**

Unless **you get total buy-in from your bosses,** they won't cooperate with and/or support your Time Locks and your Structured Time-Managed Workflow Implementation Action Plan

All of the chapters of *TBS,* including everything you learned about planning until now, has been an off-line, off-Broadway rehearsal that prepares you for this magic moment entitled the **Mutual Charter Agreement** or **MCA** *(see graphic at right).*

The MCA contains a logical if/then scenario, which, to your Time Bandit, proffers the following quid pro quo.

"If I promise you something of great value that can only come from Time Locking empowerment and enablement, then will you trust me to do so?"

Explaining the benefits of *TBS* will be easy for you, but to facilitate your first efforts, I have provided you with *TBS* benefits and features Guideline Language on Page 211. You can also find an example of an MCA at the end of this chapter.

Although MCAs are non-binding agreements between you and your management and your colleagues, once they and you execute the MCA, the rights and privileges can be enthusiastically rationalized and operationalized.

It's worth repeating: unless you get total buy-in from your bosses, they won't cooperate with and/or support your Time Locks and your Structured Time-Managed Workflow Implementation Action Plan. But if you succeed in persuading them that your plans can be responsible for generating the following benefits, you can bet your boots they'll cooperate with enthusiasm! Let's go over them.

1. Increased market share.

2. Increased share of wallet.

3. Increased customer satisfaction.

4. Increased retentions.

5. Increased personal motivation to obtain the up-skilling necessary for becoming a superior customer-centric relationship manager.

6. Firm-wide support for the new *TBS* workflow paradigm.

MUTUAL CHARTER AGREEMENT

1. WHAT IS A MUTUAL CHARTER AGREEMENT?

The Mutual Charter Agreement ("MCA") is a strategic contract entered into in good faith by and between you and your managers.

2. PURPOSE

- To achieve the mutual benefits that can be derived from "Time Locking," "Batch Processing," and "Focal Locking"
- To increase personal/corporate productivity and quality control
  - More, Better, Different, Less (MBDL Gap Analysis)
    - More of the right things
    - Implemented Better
    - Recognizing that which needs to be done Differently
    - Recognizing that which needs to be done Less or not at all

3. VISION

- Dramatically increased profitable sales revenues
- Dramatically increased service effectiveness
- Dramatically increased client satisfaction
- Dramatically increased employee job satisfaction
- Dramatically decreased employee turnover

4. MISSION

To actualize the MCA vision by developing a mutually agreed-upon Structured Time-Managed Workflow Implementation Action Plan.

In connection with the fifth benefit, if the primary objective of management's Critical Few is to maintain a competitive edge in your industry, training for up-skilling purposes is critical. But training to up-skill takes time. Your bosses will recognize that they are being asked to do something that takes time, and in their time-starved status are bound to have misgivings. So, what is one of the most important points you must make in your MCA proposal? You must credibly assert how *TBS* enables you to find that time!

After three decades of teaching management techniques for increasing productivity, including sales administration and operations, for the purposes of changing behavior, I have always used what we call the **MBDL Protocol.** MBDL stands for **More, Better, Different, Less.**

Do **More** of the right things.
Do some things **Better.**
Do some things **Differently.**
Do some things **Less** or not at all.

With more quality time, naturally you'll have time and opportunity to do **more** of the right things. Not only will you have the time to do more of the right things, but you'll have more time to do more of the right things even **better!**

When you have more time, of course you can be more analytical and thus decide whether or not a methodology for doing things **differently** is called for with respect to the behaviors you implement. Lastly, and of equal importance, you'll recognize what you should be doing **less** of or not at all.

So, as you prepare for our next exercise, let me offer these reminders from our years of experience:

● Using the MBDL Protocol, explain what you will be doing more, better, different or less, if your managers cooperate with your *TBS* approach to your workflow.

One of the most important points you must make in your MCA proposal: you must credibly assert **how *TBS* enables you to find that time!**

- Use the Guideline Language I have provided and remember that the primary purpose is to show your boss that, as a result of Time Locking, you will be able to do more of the things that generate results, such as more outbound calling, or off-site client visits.

- If applicable, in your MCA proposal, try to quantify the greater results you will achieve as a result of their cooperation. Here is an example of what I mean:

  - *"With more time, I can make 10 additional calls per day. That's 50 per week. And with a 10 percent close ratio, that equates to five new accounts that would generate X dollars per month, which could result in Y amount of incremental revenue for the firm in one year's time."*

  or...

  - *"With more time, I can help more customers per day with their service needs, resulting in X increase in service scores for our organization."*

- Anticipate every predictable objection your managers may have and remember the 4 categories and response correlators for each objection. If necessary, refer back to Chapter 5:15 for useful language for overcoming each objection.

As you prepare your MCA, **anticipate every predictable objection** your managers may have.

You are inviting people who hold great influence over your career to **join you on a remarkable path** that will make their life, and yours, "sublime."

● Remember, there is no such thing as resistance-free selling. Don't let your enthusiasm about *TBS* convince you that they will automatically match your enthusiasm.

As you develop your MCA proposal, remember to enjoy the process, because you are inviting people who hold great influence over your career to join you on a remarkable path that will make their life, and yours, "sublime."

Please prepare your own MCA proposal script and once you have role-played and rehearsed it, sit down with your manager and discuss the benefits that Time Locking can bring him, you, and the firm as a whole.

Please feel free to use the language I have provided for you in the pages to follow and modify it to fit your own personality. Once you have gained a mutual understanding with your manager, take the agreed-upon points of your proposal and formalize them in the actual MCA for execution by both parties. Make sure that your manager understands that the MCA is simply a gentlemen's agreement that is meant to encourage each of you to keep your side of the bargain. Again, use the template I have provided for the preparation of the MCA.

MCA Proposal Script Example

Initiating Process of Educating Manager

Format	Guideline Language and Key Elements
	*"I recently **read a book** entitled **TBS** and am excited **to share with you recommendations** that I believe will help us **get more control over our time** and **improve our productivity,** sales results, and even the satisfaction of our customers.* *"In TBS, **we calculated the time we lose** each day due to unplanned interruptions. I was surprised to discover that I'm losing nearly 4 hours a day, and the average for others was about 5 hours a day."*
Explain Time Locking • **What it is** • **Benefits to manager** • **Benefits to firm**	*"What's exciting is that, after quantifying time lost to unplanned interruptions, **we learned techniques** such as **Time Locking** to dramatically **reduce these interruptions.** Time Locking is where we schedule specific periods of time that **are free of interruptions** in order to focus on high-priority tasks. For example, instead of trying to get our outbound customer calls done a few minutes here and there throughout the day, **we would work out a Mutual Time Lock schedule** for our team where each of us has **dedicated time** for these important calls. This would allow us to **get more calls done,** which would **increase our sales results.*** *"We also learned how to **educate our Time Bandits,** meaning anyone who interrupts us and steals our time, so we can **be most helpful to them** and also more productive. For example, when I interrupt you while you are trying to get reports done for your manager, I'm your Time Bandit. If you had a daily Time Lock where I and my peers did not interrupt you, would it be helpful in terms of **your ability to get work done?** I'm certain we could work that out. Likewise, we could do the same for me and each of our team members.* *"Of course **our customers are our number one priority,** but they can be Time Bandits too. For example, it's hard to focus on the customer I'm meeting with when another one drops in and wants me to immediately take care of something for him. We learned how to **consultatively educate our customer Time Bandits** about the benefits to them of **setting a phone or in-person appointment** where we can devote our **undivided attention to their needs.** I tried this earlier today with our customer Bob Walters, and his reaction was very positive. I think it **made him feel special** that I set an appointment with him."*

Quantify Benefits
 	
Ask for Agreement
• Determine Implementation Action Plan
• Use appropriate communication style
  • "May I..."
  • "Thank you..."
  • "Might I suggest..."
  • "May I repeat what you said to make sure I'm clear?"
	*"In TBS we **developed a Structured Time-Managed Workflow Implementation Action Plan** that incorporates **Time Locking, Batch Processing,** and other techniques we learned. I think my plan will allow me to **get back about 10 hours a week** to focus on **high-impact activities** which I estimate **will increase my sales** results by about 20%. While each person's situation will be different, the impact of having all our team members participate in a structured time management plan would be significant. With your support I'd **like to share the benefits of mutual Time Locking** with our team and propose that we move forward with a unified plan. May we take **a few more minutes to discuss this now?"***

SAMPLE

Mutual Charter Agreement Template

1. Purpose:

To achieve the mutual benefits that can be derived from Time Locking,
Batch Processing, and Focal Locking

2. Specific Goals and Objectives:

A. To increase personal/corporate productivity and quality control

- More, Better, Different, Less (MBDL) Gap Analysis
- More of the right things
- Implemented Better
- Recognizing that which needs to be done Differently
- Recognizing that which needs to be done Less or not at all

B. To increase behavioral, quantitative, and qualitative capacities and competencies

C. To increase self-confidence, self-esteem, self-motivation, and overall job
satisfaction

D. To decrease personal distress

E. To increase customer qualitative-service-performance results

F. To mitigate the increased responsibilities of employee survivors of downsizing
(if it has occurred) by achieving the benefits of #2A-E above

G. To increase corporate profitability through increased employee/employer
performance results

H. With increased productivity will come increased profitability such that
employer/employee satisfaction will increase, leading to growth and
development for both

I. To achieve sustained behavioral and quantitative peak performance

3. Conditions of the Agreement:

A. The employer, in recognition of the employee's good intentions as set forth above, will agree to permit, accept, and encourage Time Locking.

B. The employee will demonstrate through a proof-of-concept internal pilot how and why Time Locking with Focal Locking and Batch Processing achieves #2 above.

C. With respect to the unique terminology involved (i.e., Time Locking, Focal Locking, and Batch Processing), it is the employee's total and complete responsibility to educate employer with respect to #1 and #2 above.

D. Time Locking will call for the employer to consider how to reduce the employee's interruptions. The employer will encourage and provide the means and method for colleague Mutual Time Lock Agreements. Staff meetings, like all other meetings with customers and colleagues, will be Time Locked and Batch Processed as much as possible, rather than occurring randomly.

4. Signatures

I have signed this MCA below as a record of my commitment.

APPROVED AND AGREED TO:

BY _____ DATE _____

BY _____ DATE _____

THE GLORY AND THE RESPONSIBILITY ARE YOURS

ACKNOWLEDGEMENT:

BY _____

SIGNED COPIES ARE TO BE SENT TO:

_____

_____

This MCA has been written in the third person. However, when you and your employer work together, personalize the third-person MCA by creating a first-person Agreement as follows: *"You, as my employer, and I, as your employee, agree to the following...."*

Mutual Charter Agreement Template

1. Purpose:

_____

_____

2. Specific Goals and Objectives:

_____
_____
_____
_____
_____
_____
_____
_____
_____
_____
_____
_____
_____
_____
_____
_____
_____
_____
_____
_____
_____
_____
_____
_____
_____
_____
_____

3. Conditions of the Agreement:

_____
_____
_____
_____
_____
_____
_____
_____
_____
_____
_____
_____
_____
_____
_____
_____
_____
_____
_____

4. Signatures

I have signed this MCA below as a record of my commitment.

APPROVED AND AGREED TO:

BY _____ DATE _____

BY _____ DATE _____

THE GLORY AND THE RESPONSIBILITY ARE YOURS

ACKNOWLEDGEMENT:

BY _____

SIGNED COPIES ARE TO BE SENT TO:

_____
_____

CHAPTER

12:30

The On-Line Application Period

Selling, negotiating, or persuading will never be a natural behavior, and we will always be subjected to **possible rejection and failure.**

In Cohen Brown sales and service sessions around the world, you often hear our facilitators say, *"The more sweat on the training field, the less blood on the battle field."* In that regard, I have always believed that all training is worthless (even what can be taught through intense role-playing and a variety of exercises (or workshops)) if the lessons are not converted into real-world action within 48 hours of the training.

Rather than leaving individual participants to fend for themselves upon their return from training, we always provide our students with a systematized methodology with qualitative and quantitative tracking along with behavioral coaching to assist them with the implementation of the behaviors they have just learned.

Here is why:

Selling, negotiating, or persuading will never be a natural behavior, and we will always be subjected to possible rejection and failure. Acceptance of this given reality is never comfortable.

And although at Cohen Brown we proclaim that *"professionals act as they must, not as they feel,"* we have discovered that it's typically hard on your own to overcome the discomfort and apply all that you have learned thus far reading this book.

For that reason, we created the **On-Line Application Period** or, as we commonly refer to it, **OLAP.**

Here's how it worked for my sales training courses.

When the training participant came to a classroom and was told what the sales training would cover, they were also told that, rather than lasting for a day, it would last for 11 days. One day in the classroom, 10 days in the real world.

I explained to the participants that pedagogically I could teach them all the didactics they would need, which would include intense role-playing as a means of getting the feeling for what the customer might say or do when they hear the initial sales pitch.

In our Scripting Clinics, we not only taught the participants what to say, we taught them how to say what to say, and then we taught them how to deal with objections.

Through role-playing and Objection Clinics, we predicted all of the objections that might be raised by a prospect or customer, and we trained the class on what things to say and how to say those things to overcome objections.

Nevertheless, when the training was over, we also said it was absolutely critical that the participant get on the telephone or be prepared to interface with their customers using what they just learned within 48 hours; otherwise, as I said before, the training would have been a total waste of time.

I also realized that while we could teach them what to say in the classroom, the one thing we could not teach them was experience. Experience comes from doing, not just knowing. So I insisted, with the support of their managers and team leaders, that they begin to use what they learned off-line, on-line; hence OLAP was born.

At one of my early banking clients, Security Pacific National Bank (SPNB), the Wealth Management division's personnel handled some of the wealthiest people in California, and the trust officers

Experience comes from doing, not just knowing. So I insisted, with the support of their managers and team leaders, that they begin to use what they learned off-line, on-line; hence OLAP was born.

and investment management specialists, to say the least, were terrified. They used to say to me, *"Ed, to pick up the phone to work my book of accounts with these clients, is like picking up an 800-pound gorilla."*

You see, my trainees suffered from what I referred to as a middle-class mentality. After all what could a banker tell these wealthy individuals about their own business that they didn't already know?

For that reason, when they were required to do a financial needs analysis profile over the phone and ask for pertinent financial information with a view towards gathering assets that they could then manage, because of fear of rejection and fear of failure, it was terrifying to them.

None of this deterred the then-Executive Vice President and my good friend, Bob Boyles, who was told by his boss that he was looking for 30–50% growth for Wealth Management in the next 12 months.

To help Bob, we perfected OLAP in such a way that, within what I refer to as the first OLAP 10-day hiatus (the ten days after the classroom training), the trainees were required to cross-pollinate their victories and failures. On the 11th day, they were thrilled to report immense successes, thus motivating each other.

Bob and I conducted a number of other OLAPs. This went on to become a way of life at SPNB

My terrified trainees would say, *"Ed, to pick up the phone to work my book of accounts with these clients, is like picking up an 800-pound gorilla."*

and, within six months, the results in Bob's own words are below:

"In the first year after we implemented Cohen Brown, revenues doubled. In the second year, revenues quadrupled; which was phenomenal. And then in the third year, we more than doubled our revenues again, off a much higher base."

The goals and objectives of the OLAP, therefore, are to carry the skills and behaviors that commenced in the training session into a real-world setting.

Look, I know you're reading a book, not sitting in my STWM class. So I want to pause here and make a distinction for you. You might be reading this book simply as an individual wanting to recapture precious time and lead a better life accordingly. If so, great, the rest of this chapter may not be applicable to you.

However, if you want to embed in your organization the lessons of this book with other members of your team or with your entire organization by having others read *TBS,* then I would do the following OLAP steps exactly as noted below.

By doing so managers can:

- Exponentially improve results
- Increase front-line management engagement and coaching
- Accomplish granular cross-pollination of technique-specific best practices
- Provide additional motivation for becoming the Best of the Best

Before training begins, managers should be the first to participate in the formal training and the On-Line Application Period. Then they will cascade the training and the On-Line Application Period down the line.

Before the formal training, there are five infrastructure roll-out steps.

Step 1

Determine the critical behavior that, if implemented more frequently and with better quality, would have a significant, positive impact on results. Once the critical behavior has been determined, schedule training.

Step 2

Determine the behaviors and the expectations for implementation:
- For example: fine-tune your Structured Time-Managed Workflow Implementation Action Plan.
- Meet with your manager to share your *TBS* and Time Locking experiences, including the results of your Time Lost

My trainees suffered from what I referred to as a **middle-class mentality.** After all what could a banker tell these wealthy individuals about their own business that they didn't already know?

Participate in debriefing(s) to **share your experiences and results** in implementing *TBS* and celebrate successes.

Calculations and your action plan. Share your proposal for mutual Time Locking, including benefits to your manager and the organization, and gain the support of your manager to proceed.

● Meet with your colleagues to share *TBS* experiences and educate them as appropriate. Gain their commitment to mutual Time Locking.

● Implement techniques learned in *TBS* including:
  ● Time Locking
  ● Focal Locking through The Mental Hygiene Process
  ● Batch Processing
  ● Planning for Hard vs. Easy
  ● Prioritization Techniques
  ● Scripting to Educate Time Bandits
  ● Overcoming Time Bandit Objections

● Identify Time Bandits with whom you can enter into a Mutual Time Lock Agreement and approach them with the goal of reaching an agreement.

● Participate in debriefing(s) to share your experiences and results in implementing *TBS* and celebrate successes. This will also be an opportunity to surface and resolve any challenges you may have encountered during implementation. Be prepared to discuss what objections you heard from your Time Bandits and how you overcame them.

● Prepare for the debriefings by:
  ● Recording details about what you implement, and notes about your experiences including key successes and challenges.
  ● Noting how many hours you save per day/week based on implementation of your Structured Time-Managed Workflow Implementation Action Plan and how this positively impacts your ability to accomplish key tasks and increases your performance results.

In preparation for your participation or leadership of the OLAP debriefing(s), take notes (or have your staff take notes) regarding your experiences and results to share with your colleagues. Include specifics such as what you did (including when and how), what worked best, and challenges (including if you overcame them and how).

Take notes (or have your staff take notes) regarding your experiences and results to share with your colleagues.

Time Locking

_____

_____

_____

Batch Processing

_____

_____

_____

Hard vs. Easy

_____

_____

_____

Prioritization Techniques

_____

_____

_____

Scripting to Educate Time Bandits

_____

_____

_____

Distress Management

_____

_____

_____

How much time have you gained back, and how this has this improved your performance?

Also note successes and benefits you are experiencing from implementation of *TBS*, including time you have gained back, and how this has improved your performance.

Key Successes

_____
_____
_____

Challenges/Solutions

_____
_____
_____

Approximate hours/day/week personally gained back based on implementation of *TBS*

_____
_____
_____

High-priority tasks/activities you are able to do more of (or get done) as a result of having gained back time through *TBS*

_____
_____

Increase in performance results as a result of being able to accomplish high-priority activities

_____
_____

Other benefits experienced with *TBS* (for yourself, your clients/prospects, and your team/organization)

_____
_____
_____

Step 3

Establish the length of the On-Line Application Period (working days/weeks). Typically, the length of an On-Line Application Period is 10 to 14 working days. Regardless of the length of the OLAP, immediate managers should follow up daily, and higher-level managers should follow up weekly.

Step 4

For motivational purposes, **determine whether behavioral and monetary goals** will be published. If so, when and how? Publish goals, commitments, and results electronically to increase the On-Line Application Period participants' motivation, positive reinforcement, and accountability while avoiding management abdication. For example, on an (electronic) leader board or one on one.

Step 5

Schedule debriefing calls at the midpoint of the On-Line Application Period (or earlier as needed).

Publish goals, commitments, and results electronically to increase the On-Line Application Period participants' motivation, positive reinforcement, and accountability while avoiding management abdication.

the Times

theTIMES.com

$1.00 DESIGNATED AREAS HIGHER

HE HITS HIS GOALS!

At the conclusion of the formal training, **use On-Line Application Period templates** to carefully explain On-Line Application Period expectations with template protocols.

There are 3 steps during the formal training session.

Step 1

Briefly announce that there will be an On-Line Application Period.

- To avoid distraction during the training session, do not share any On-Line Application Period details.

Step 2

At the conclusion of the formal training, **use On-Line Application Period templates** to carefully explain On-Line Application Period expectations with template protocols.

- What are the On-Line Application Period behavioral tasks?
- Who is responsible?
- When do the tasks begin?
- When will the On-Line Application Period be finished, and when will participants be expected to perform the behavioral tasks with less monitoring and coaching?
- What are the roles of the facilitator and the role models?
- What is the tracking methodology for the commitments made?

Step 3

Explain that there will be a midpoint debriefing; announce the date and time and explain that the midpoint debriefing includes:

- Debriefing qualitative and quantitative results
- Sharing successes, challenges, and solutions
- Reinforcing critical techniques
- Motivating participants to continue implementing behaviors

Be prepared for team members' objections to having the OLAP.

There are 2 steps during the On-Line Application Period (hiatus).

Step 1

Develop and/or oversee the execution of Structured Time-Managed Workflow Implementation Action Plans.

Step 2

Increase positive reinforcement and motivation by

- Setting behavioral and related metric goals and publishing these goals

- Conducting observation and coaching with skill-building in the field, which increases behavioral accuracy, self-confidence, self-esteem, and job satisfaction, and diminishes fear of rejection and fear of failure
- Conducting contests with reward and recognition
- Providing accountability as needed

Midway through an On-Line Application Period

Conduct the midpoint debriefing, including:

- Debriefing of qualitative and quantitative results
- Sharing successes, challenges, and solutions
- Reinforcing critical techniques
- Motivating participants to continue implementing behaviors

Post-On-Line Application Period Debriefing

After an On-Line Application Period, **participants gather to share and discuss** their experiences. For example, if the On-Line Application Period is 10 working days, on the 11th day there is a formal face-to-face or teleconference gathering of participants.

This post-On-Line Application Period training is critical because it will inform management as to whether or not the formal training generated desired results and, if so, to what extent, or if not, why not.

During the next formal face-to-face or teleconference training, the following can occur:

- The training participants cross-pollinate victories, which helps motivate others.
- The participants share their concern over objections raised during the On-Line Application Period that were not covered in the formal training.
- The facilitator runs additional scriptwriting clinics to overcome any new objections.
- Participants reacquaint themselves with content from the formal training.
- Facilitators run pop quizzes to make sure that the participants are Clear, Capable, and Motivated.
- Additional role-playing is conducted based on the above.

After an On-Line Application Period, **participants gather to share and discuss** their experiences.

Congratulations

There you have it.
Your very own *Time Bandit Solution* for making your life better. Your own black belt in *TBS*.

I know you were delighted to discover that this was no ordinary "time management" treatise, urging you to get serious and get organized. Instead you got a practical, insightful study in interpersonal relationship management.

Instead of organizing techniques, you learned **ten major lessons** that will help you seize your life back from the interruption culture.

1 If you are like most time-strapped people, you were losing 40–60% of your precious time to interruptions – things that stole your time for **no good reason**. Even if it was just one hour a day, imagine having five free hours every week to use in your most important pursuits!

2 You learned that in our belt-tightening economy, with layoffs and hiring freezes, time pressures were only going to be greater, and you will feel more stress, **no matter what your personality type is.**

3 You learned the **five insidious ways interruptions steal your precious time,** all while acculturating you to tolerate interruptions and your Time Bandits.

4 You learned how **you can prevent interruptions** without damaging your relationships with your Time Bandits, who are often your colleagues, bosses, and clients, through Time Locking.

5 **Through Focal Locking,** with its many helpful concentration techniques, you learned to conquer your worst Time Bandit, yourself.

6 You developed **new arts and skills** for helping your Time Bandits appreciate your new approach for managing your time and actively cooperate with you.

7 **You overcame a great fear – your fear of their objections** – and learned to welcome their objections as the path to persuading them.

8 You learned how to **distinguish your Critical Few tasks from your Minor Many,** to separate the hard ones from the easy, to identify tasks for Batch Processing, and to recognize the best times for doing different kinds of work.

9 You learned how to **observe planning protocols** when you plan your activities, so that you could put all these new lessons to work – and you even found surplus time as promised.

10 And, finally, you learned how to **take accountability for these lessons** and make sure they become embedded in your day-to-day life.

You learned **ten major lessons** that will help you seize your life back from the interruption culture.

Imagine how much smoother
your Time Lock proposals would go. What if your boss, and your boss's boss, all the way up the line, also became dedicated Time Lockers and Focal Lockers?

I think I know how you feel right now. You're thrilled to have learned from this book how you can change your life, reclaim your own precious time, and enjoy peace of mind where stress used to prevail. You're excited and confident, and you should be.

However, these lessons were learned by you alone. There is a magic to working with the critical mass of your colleagues where the power of brainstorming in a room can help the entire process of *TBS* come to life.

Imagine how much smoother your Time Lock proposals would go – how much support you would have. What if your boss, and your boss's boss, all the way up the line, also became dedicated Time Lockers and Focal Lockers?

That magic is felt by all of our Structured Time and Workflow Management (STWM) participants.

By taking part in STWM, you would enjoy having the learning "come alive" in a classroom setting. Trust me, I'm not going back on my belief in the beauty of solitude. Great work does happen by committed people working alone and uninterrupted. But book-learning is greatly enhanced and enriched by leader-led communal education – that is, in a classroom setting.

With STWM, you would become part of a team that works from the same playbook. Instead of just you working wiser, your whole group will become a cohesive group, working in sync, getting more work done while enjoying it more. For our clients who have experienced STWM, their employees consider STWM participation one of their most valued perks!

So I will close here with three final takeaways for you:

● A plan only works if you work it.
● Creativity without implementation is worthless.
● Execution is the chariot of genius.

Old habits will beckon. Maybe you will find yourself, in a weak moment, tempted to indulge a persistent Time Bandit. You might let your guard down and decide to wing it next week instead of planning it. You may wish to abandon a Time Lock when the going gets hard, or you might knee-jerk a decision without the benefit of Quiet Time. Whatever your besetting habit was before you read this book, you are still vulnerable to "snapping back" to it – that's what we call the Rubber Band Principle.

Keep this book at hand for those moments. If necessary, turn to your Implementation Action Plan near the end of Chapter 11:30, where you first saw your glorious week carefully plotted out with time for everything on your plate, and remember how invincible you felt then.

And take to heart these two statements from my friend and client Sol Levy, whose company is a much-satisfied user of STWM, the methodology that underpins this book.

His first statement is a warning: *"When you have deep-seated, almost unconscious behaviors that cause problems, you might as well be talking about a disease, or an addiction. Sheer will or command is not going to solve it. You need a plan and you need to work the plan."*

But, as stated in the Introduction, Sol's second statement is inspirational: *"There are two ways you can stretch your life: adding extra years, or getting more out of life every day. Our people are learning to get more out of life every day – not just at work but in how they live their lives."*

Have a great life, *TBS* expert!

Whatever your besetting habit was before you read this book, you are still vulnerable to "snapping back" to it – that's what we call the **Rubber Band Principle.**

Glossary

80/20 Rule (Pareto's Principle): 80% of your results come from 20% of your activities.

AIAI: Aggravation, Irritation, Anger, and Impatience.

AOC: Administration, operations, and compliance issues/problems/tasks.

Batch Processing: A time-management technique whereby similar tasks are performed as a group, rather than being performed randomly or as they occur (e.g., writing reports, processing e-mail). Batch Processing improves both effectiveness and efficiency by eliminating false starts and increases focus.

Behavioral Planning: Creating a step-by-step implementation plan associated with the behaviors needed to accomplish the goals of the plan.

Book of Accounts: A portfolio of clients.

Cause: Something that produces a result or consequence.

Client: Anyone who needs your support, whether internal or external.

Clinics: A leadership and management activity used by managers to prepare team members for any form of verbal interaction; develop first-person, personalized scripts; and rehearse what to say in given situations. See also Objections Clinics and Scriptwriting Clinics.

Communication Arts and Skills: Communication has two components: skill and art. The scripts and objection responses covered are the skill. How you say what you say is the art.

Constructive Acceptance: Accepting that which you cannot change.

Counterpunching: A term taken from boxing; the highly effective counterpunching technique replaces a negative mindset with positive affirmations, which neutralize the power of negative thinking.

Critical Few: In terms of time management and based on the 80/20 Rule, these are the 20% of tasks or functions to perform to achieve success as compared to the less critical (i.e., the 80% or the Minor Many) tasks. See also Minor Many.

Use this glossary to **familiarize yourself with terms** in *The Time Bandit Solution.*

D-H

DERSSIM Logic System: Define, Effects, Reasons, Solutions, Solution Implementation Methodology

Distress: Levels of stress that cause us to lose self-control and make us feel overwhelmed.

Do-Over: Doing a task again to correct errors.

Effect: Something brought about by, or as a result of, distress.

Egalitarian Time-Management Behavior Phenomenon: The mentality of treating the execution of all tasks with equal importance.

Energy Vampire: People with a negative bent that sap your energy for doing your work.

Eu-stress: Positive stress.

Executional Excellence (E^2): Mastery x Consistency = Executional Excellence. Mastery is great skillfulness and knowledge; Consistency is reliability and repeatability; and Executional Excellence is performing to the highest standards.

Feel/Felt/Found Principle: A consultative technique for handling certain categories of objections. A statement of reassurance is structured to let the client know that others have been in a similar situation and that their concerns were resolved satisfactorily:

1. **Feel** – represents the need to empathize with the objection, *"I understand how you feel."*

2. **Felt** – demonstrates feelings held by clients in similar situations and, using the past tense, indicates that other clients went forward. Adding the word "initially" to "felt" enhances the impression that the objection was overcome and that other clients proceeded. *"In fact, initially, most of my clients/prospects felt just like you."*

3. **Found** – reveals to the prospect or client the reason he or she should go forward as others have. *"But they have found..."*

Focal Locking: The ability to concentrate and stay on task while you're in a Time Lock.

Given Reality Test: Understanding the effects of not solving a problem.

Goal: Provides a reason for action and clarifies the team's direction and expectations. Goals can be performance, action, monetary, and behavioral.

The Highest Correlators of Psychotherapeutic Techniques:
- Transcending the Environment
- Constructive Acceptance
- Visualizing the Ideal Self
- Positive Affirmation

- Psychological Counterpunching
- Changing Your Mental Computer

Importance vs. Urgency Prioritization Grid: A grid that helps to prioritize tasks. The grid is based on the following definitions:

- Importance = our perspective; things that are important to us.
- Urgency = others' perspectives; items that are important to others are interpreted as being urgent.

Interruption: In business, anything that disrupts workflow and concentration.

Market Share: The quantity of clients in your market as compared to your competitors.

MBDL: More, Better, Different, Less
1. More of the right things
2. Implemented Better
3. Recognizing that which needs to be done Differently
4. Recognizing that which needs to be done Less or not at all

Medical Model: Like medical doctors, sales professionals proceed in a systematic fashion for the benefit of their clients/prospects. By thinking of yourself as a "physician," you can better serve your clients by...
1. Focusing on understanding what is going on with the person (symptom).
2. Making a diagnosis once you have identified a cause.
3. Following up with a treatment recommendation; either implement the recommendation or refer it.

The concept of symptoms, diagnosis, and treatment correlates directly to the effects, causes, and solutions for distress.

Mental Hygiene Process: The Mental Hygiene Process is a methodology to overcome Mental Leakage. The process is composed of techniques with very defined, learnable skills and steps and is designed to become as habitual and natural as the physical hygiene process.

Mental Leakage: Giving in to self-created interruptions, like emails, voicemails, YouTube.

Minor Many: In terms of time management and based on the 80/20 Rule, these are the 80% of tasks or functions that are not critical to achieving success as compared to the more critical tasks (i.e., the 20% or the Critical Few). See also Critical Few.

Momentum Loss: Interruptions break the flow developed by performing similar tasks continuously.

I-M

M-P

Multi-tasking: Performing more than one task or behavior at a time.

Mutual Charter Agreement (MCA): A nonbinding agreement between members of an organization, such as an employer and employee, that enables Time Locking and Batch Processing.

Mutual Time Lock Agreement: An agreement between two or more colleagues that establishes, in writing, who will do what for whom and when this will occur.

Ninja: People who intentionally or unintentionally resist organization change, including positive ones.

Non-Interactive Environmental Issues: Situations over which you have no control:

- Physical facilities
- Policy rules and regulations
- Administrative, operations, and compliance issues

Objection: Any response other than a "yes." Objections, which can include questions or requests for information, are usually an expression of interest and show that the person is listening.

Objection(s) Categorizer and Response Correlators:

Objections Categories	Response Correlators
1. No Need	1. Probe, Second Opinion
2. Distrust	2. Feel/Felt/Found
3. Inconvenience	3. To Talk: Reschedule To Implement: Feel/Felt/Found; or Pilot
4. Don't Understand	4. Educate

Objections Clinic: A clinic specifically conducted to prepare team members to respond to objections, concerns, and resistances. Because objections are the critical path to the close, all objections—including unexpressed objections—must be uncovered and resolved. Responses to objections are rehearsed and perfected.

On-Line Application Period: A process that combines coaching and accountability to provide individuals in the organization with real-world experience for the application of classroom learning. On-Line Application features on-the-job implementation of the skills and techniques that were learned in the classroom. It is supervised and goal-based, and results are tracked. On-Line Application is generally followed by classroom debriefing of the results achieved and successes and challenges encountered.

Pilot: An experimental or trial undertaking prior to full-scale operation or use: a pilot project.

Planning Protocol: A series of questions used to simplify planning.

- What means what is the task that you're planning to achieve?
- How means how will you achieve those tasks?
- Who means, other than yourself, who else will you be relying on to achieve these tasks?
- How Many means how many of these tasks must be implemented to achieve your goals?
- By When means by when are you planning to get started with your task, and by when will you be finished?

Positive Affirmation: A technique used to program the subconscious mind to effect change by repeating (or meditating on) a key phrase to bring about the desired outcome

Positive Self-Visualization: The ability to visualize your "ideal self" and the goals you hope to achieve despite challenges, conflicts, and adversity.

Quid Pro Quo: Something that is given or taken in return for something else; substitute.

Quiet Time: The predecessor to Time Locking.

Scripting Checklist
1. Convey key points to the Time Bandit.
2. Identify Big 5 headlines. Rank them in priority order.
3. Please conform to these rules:
   - No hyperbole (truth only, please)
   - Researched and factual
   - Simple, clear and articulate
   - Pre-position and encourage questions and objections
   - Conversational (speak from the heart)
4. Your list should contain the basic key elements:
   - Although you are facing a critical deadline, you will help the Time Bandit with his/her needs.
   - Explain the purpose and mutual benefits of your Time Locking goals and plans.
   - Because of your current deadlines, seek concurrence for a formal in-person or telephone meeting time.
   - Thank the client for his/her understanding and set the appointment.

Please personalize the Guideline Language and, in doing so, remember the truth always wins and speak from your heart.

CONTINUED ON THE NEXT PAGE

P-S

5. Rehearse, rehearse, rehearse.
6. Incorporate the five critically important phases into your presentation:
   - Intro/Entry Lines
   - Time Lock Solution Needs
   - Response to Objections
   - Exit Lines
   - The Close

Scriptwriting Clinic: A clinic specifically conducted for team members to learn how to handle situations that require verbal interaction. Team members learn how to write the best possible first-person scripts in the shortest period of time. After being written, the script is rehearsed and perfected.

Share of Wallet: The number of products your clients buy.

Skill Building: Managers assist team members in developing their skills.

Structured Time & Workflow Management: An ongoing process that focuses on learning how to use structured time-management techniques to recover time that is unnecessarily wasted and to utilize that time surplus to implement critical initiatives with Executional Excellence, increased productivity, reduced stress, and greater overall job satisfaction.

Style: The art form of communication.

Style Rules:
1. Speak from the heart, not just from the brain.
2. Put a smile in your voice, and put a smile in your heart.
3. Speak at a tempo that is natural for you, so you don't sound like you're reading.
4. Use communication etiquette techniques.
5. Use effective body language.
6. Use effective listening techniques.

Survivor: A person who outlived the financial crisis/layoffs.

Time Bandit: A person or an event that interrupts you and "steals" your time.

Time Locking: Creating time periods which are totally freed of interruptions (other than emergencies) for the purpose of absolute focus on specific tasks.

Time Lock Sign: A sign placed in an individual's workplace that communicates to others that the person is not to be interrupted unless it is a predefined emergency.

Time-Loss Factors: Unplanned interruptions cause restarts and momentum loss, which in turn can cause mistakes, do-overs, and distress, resulting in massive amounts of wasted time.
1. Interruptions
2. Restarts
3. Momentum Loss
4. Quality Control Errors Resulting in Do-Overs
5. Distress Manifestations

Top Ten Effects Caused by Interruption-Driven Distress:
1. Hopelessness
2. De-motivated
3. Mental & Physical Exhaustion
4. Rejected
5. Low Self-Esteem
6. Frustrated
7. Insecure
8. Confused
9. Unappreciated
10. Misunderstood

Type A, B, & C Personalities: Despite the fact that each personality type suffers from the same causes and effects of time-management pressure, the levels of distress that each of them experience are completely different.

- **Type A:** Live in almost constant distress that there's not enough time to get their stuff done
- **Type B:** Confident there's always plenty of time and often take on more than they can do and then struggle with deadlines
- **Type C:** Live in almost constant distress that there's not enough time to achieve perfection

Appendix

Here are additional helpful grids, worksheets and samples mentioned in the text. For more information on each graphic, please see the accompanying page number reference.

Mutual Time Lock Agreement

The Mutual Time Lock Agreement sets down in writing the agreement by team members, colleagues, and possibly even your managers on how they will react and respond to Time Locking.

Identifying Agreement Partners Worksheet

WORKSHEET INSTRUCTIONS:

1. Identify the individuals with whom you want to enter into an agreement. Take into consideration team members, colleagues, and managers.
2. Document the reason you want to enter into an agreement with them.

INDIVIDUAL	REASON FOR AGREEMENT

See page 102

CONTINUED ON THE NEXT PAGE

Mutual Time Lock Agreement CONTINUED

Mutual Time Lock Agreement Terms & Conditions Checklist

Develop the details of the checklist based on the specific terms of the agreement you want to include. Some details have been included for reference, but you can add your own in the blank areas.

INDICATE NON-NEGOTIABLE OR COMPULSORY COMPONENTS WITH CHECK MARKS.

PLAN TO INCLUDE	DID INCLUDE	COMPONENT
○	○	**Stated and agreed-upon purpose of agreement ("Vision"):**
○	○	Commitment to increased client service
○	○	Increased benefits to clients, team members, and Time Locking partner
○	○	
○	○	**Stated specific goals and objectives:**
○	○	To implement Time Locking reciprocity
○	○	
○	○	**Stated terms and conditions of the agreement:**
○	○	Commitment to respecting each other's Time Locks
○	○	Proposed days of the week and times of day for Time Locks
○	○	Agreement about how we will communicate our Time Locks to other people
○	○	Agreement about our definition of what constitutes an emergency (i.e., situations when a Time Lock can be interrupted)
○	○	
○	○	**Offered to sign and date the agreement:**
○	○	

CONTINUED ON THE NEXT PAGE

Mutual Time Lock Agreement CONTINUED

Mutual Time Lock Agreement Proposal Template

Purpose

"The purpose of this Mutual Time Lock Agreement is to establish how we initiate, react to, and reciprocate Time Locking tasks."

Specific Goals and Objectives

"Since my team members, managers, colleagues, and clients are important to me, I realize that I cannot serve all needs and requests as they arise. I need to be able to concentrate on my Critical Few and Minor Many tasks in a structured, time-managed manner."

"Therefore, to promote Executional Excellence, I formally express the terms of my time-managed program as follows."

The four goals: (change these goals to meet the needs of your agreement)

 "Indicate that I am Time Locking."

 "Create Mutual Time Lock Agreements for my most important relationships—my team members, colleagues, managers, and clients."

 "Communicate the terms under which I can be interrupted while Time Locking."

 "Formally commit to assisting colleagues, managers, or team members by temporarily carrying out their tasks while they are Time Locking."

CONTINUED ON THE NEXT PAGE

Mutual Time Lock Agreement CONTINUED

Identify Conditions of the Agreement

ENTER ANY CONDITIONS OF THE AGREEMENT:

 We commit ourselves to providing Executional Excellence by following the tenets of structured time management.

 We will attain and sustain momentum at peak performance levels whenever possible.

_____

_____

_____

_____

_____

Create a formal Time Locking schedule.

ENTER THE DAY, TIME, AND DURATION OF REGULARLY SCHEDULED PERIODS
WHEN YOU WILL TIME LOCK TO COMPLETE BATCH PROCESSING TASKS.

_____

_____

_____

_____

_____

_____

Formalize unscheduled Time Locking terms and conditions.

ENTER THE TERMS UNDER WHICH YOU CAN BE INTERRUPTED, E.G., EMERGENCY SITUATIONS
OR A MAJOR CHANGE IN THE GOAL OF A TASK OR INITIATIVE.

_____

_____

_____

_____

_____

CONTINUED ON THE NEXT PAGE

Mutual Time Lock Agreement CONTINUED

Expect the following tasks to be covered while Time Locking

LIST THE TASKS TO BE ACCOMPLISHED BY THE PERSON OR PERSONS ENTERING
INTO THIS CONTRACT WITH YOU.

_____

_____

_____

_____

_____

_____

_____

_____

_____

_____

_____

Identify Tasks to Reciprocate

LIST THE TASKS YOU WILL COVER FOR THE PERSON OR PERSONS ENTERING
INTO THIS CONTRACT WITH YOU.

_____

_____

_____

_____

_____

_____

_____

_____

_____

_____

_____

CONTINUED ON THE NEXT PAGE

Mutual Time Lock Agreement CONTINUED

Obtain Signatures

I have signed this Mutual Time Lock Agreement below as a record
of my commitment.

APPROVED AND AGREED TO:

YOUR SIGNATURE

DATE

TEAM MEMBER'S SIGNATURE

DATE

ACKNOWLEDGMENT:

MANAGER OF TEAM MEMBER INITIATING THIS AGREEMENT

DATE

Signed copies are to be sent to each of the team members named
in this agreement and their managers.

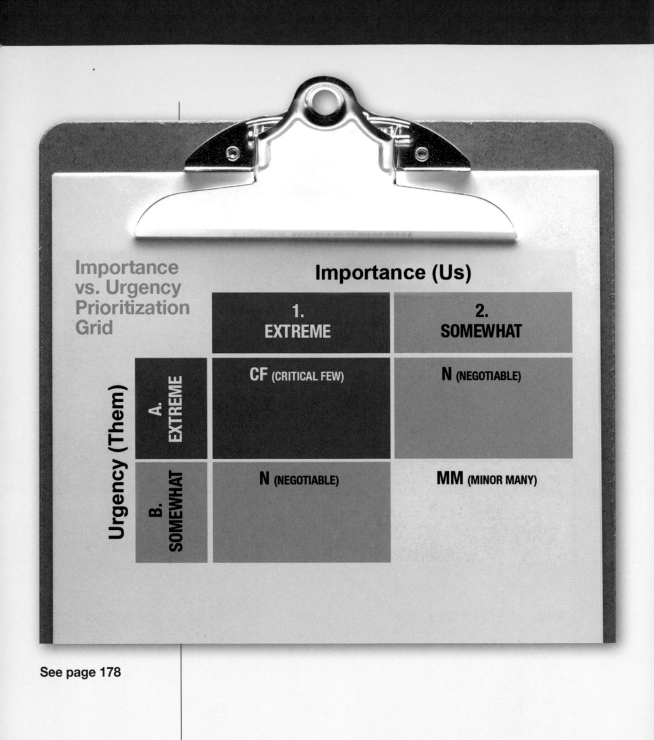

Importance vs. Urgency Prioritization Grid

Importance (Us)

	1. **EXTREME**	**2.** **SOMEWHAT**
A. **EXTREME**	CF (CRITICAL FEW)	N (NEGOTIABLE)
B. **SOMEWHAT**	N (NEGOTIABLE)	MM (MINOR MANY)

Urgency (Them)

See page 178

TIME-MANAGEMENT WORKSHEET

TASK	CF/MM	FREQ	BATCH	H/E	DOW	TIME LOCK	TIME NEEDED	WHO

See page 181

Mutual Charter Agreement Template

1. Purpose:

_____
_____

2. Specific Goals and Objectives:

_____
_____
_____
_____
_____
_____
_____
_____
_____
_____
_____
_____
_____
_____
_____
_____
_____
_____
_____
_____
_____
_____
_____
_____
_____
_____
_____
_____
_____
_____
_____

See pages 214-215

3. Conditions of the Agreement:

_____
_____
_____
_____
_____
_____
_____
_____
_____
_____
_____
_____
_____
_____
_____

4. Signatures

I have signed this MCA below as a record of my commitment.

APPROVED AND AGREED TO:

BY _____ DATE _____

BY _____ DATE _____

THE GLORY AND THE RESPONSIBILITY ARE YOURS

ACKNOWLEDGEMENT:

BY _____

SIGNED COPIES ARE TO BE SENT TO:

_____
_____

Permissions

Selected photos shown in *The Time Bandit Solution* are used with permission. Additional credits listed below.

PAGE	IMAGE	PHOTOGRAPHER	SOURCE
9	82556845	Pixland	Thinkstock
10	87814496	Jupiterimages	Thinkstock
12	97801688	Rangizzz	Shutterstock
14	78253320	Goodshoot	Thinkstock
16	SKD188173SDC	Stockbyte	Thinkstock
19	174910815	CBS Photo Archive	Getty Images
22	109504499	Dreamerve	Shutterstock
22	84707065	CBS Photo Archive	Getty Images
23	7586082	Swilmor	iStock
25	200288295-001	Ryan McVay	Thinkstock
26	DV071045A	Stockbyte	Thinkstock
27	70477243	Brian Goodman	Shutterstock
29	8065798	Brand X Pictures	Thinkstock
30	E014289	Stockbyte	Thinkstock
31	87814496	Jupiterimages	Thinkstock
32	89794780	Jupiterimages	Thinkstock
33	81284272	Comstock Images	Thinkstock
34	78292789	Goodshoot	Thinkstock
35	165577	Russell	Getty Images
36	92826542	Photos.com	Thinkstock
37	76037243	Jack Hollingsworth	Thinkstock
38	Laptop image	Stan Hulen	Hulen Design
39	80608782	Creatas Images	Thinkstock
40	200488260-001	Adam Taylor	Thinkstock
41	87501641	Jupiterimages	Thinkstock
49	117790654	Beeside Photography	Shutterstock
51	139832689	Markus Beck	Shutterstock
53	RR020483	Roger Ressmeyer	Corbis Images
55	80605808	Brand X Pictures	Thinkstock
55	STK18770DLE	Stockbyte	Thinkstock
55	83253884	Jupiterimages	Thinkstock
57	DV153154A	Stockbyte	Thinkstock
58	78377909	Jupiterimages	Thinkstock
61	Family photo	Personal collection	Edward Brown
62	92822577	Photos.com/Getty	Thinkstock
63	85354796	Gilles Petard	Getty Images
63	74297376	Michael Ochs/Stringer	Getty Images
63	23564906	Hemera Technologies	Thinkstock
64	124091059	Nito	Shutterstock
65	Various photos	Personal collection	Edward Brown
65	87548162	Photos.com	Thinkstock
66	RBRB_2841	Photodisc	Thinkstock
67	78484526	Comstock	Thinkstock
68	Portrait	Personal collection	Edward Brown
69	74275740	Michael Ochs	Getty Images
71	200467136-001	Thomas Northcut	Thinkstock
72	78460671	Comstock	Thinkstock
74	87970927	Zedcor / Getty Images	Thinkstock
74	SKD188535SDC	Stockbyte	Thinkstock
75	200355237	Marilli Forasteri	Thinkstock
76	SKD181070SDC	George Doyle & Ciaran Griffin	Thinkstock
76	78395197	Brand X Pictures	Thinkstock
77	78291409	Goodshoot	Thinkstock
78	78291023	Goodshoot	Thinkstock
79	200327116-001	Thomas Northcut	Thinkstock
79	83323369	Boris15	Shutterstock
79	87516258	Jupiterimages	Thinkstock
80	86489168	Jupiterimages	Thinkstock
81	E010259	Stockbyte	Thinkstock
82	78488575	Comstock	Thinkstock
83	MEDFR03516	Medioimages/Photodisc	Thinkstock
84	BES_089	Stockbyte	Thinkstock
86	DV141035B	Stockbyte	Thinkstock
87	76756441	Creatas	Thinkstock
88	SKD188173SDC	Stockbyte	Thinkstock
88	STK178203RKE	Stockbyte	Thinkstock
89	Portrait	Personal collection	Edward Brown
89	DV255003	Digital Vision	Thinkstock
90	DV071011A	Stockbyte	Thinkstock
91	87453478	Ablestock.com	Thinkstock

PAGE	IMAGE	PHOTOGRAPHER	SOURCE
92	99104240	Warren Goldswain	Shutterstock
93	92914715	Comstock Images	Thinkstock
94	9539596	Gordan	Shutterstock
96	25559764	Gajus	iStock
97	87539825	Jupiterimages	Thinkstock
98	STK116337RKE	George Doyle	Thinkstock
101	STK318010RKN	Ciaran Griffin	Thinkstock
104	86491512	Dynamic Graphics	Thinkstock
105	CC000581	Jason Reed	Thinkstock
105	DV1940089	Digital Vision	Thinkstock
106	92836796	Photos.com	Thinkstock
107	87684491	Hemera Technologies	Thinkstock
108	78320900	Brand X Pictures	Thinkstock
109	104553509	Auremar	Shutterstock
110	83252596	Jupiterimages	Thinkstock
111	140868285	NBC Universal	Getty Images
112	89835559	Pressmaster	Shutterstock
114	86523657	Jupiterimages	Thinkstock
117	STK19951BOJ	Stockbyte	Thinkstock
118	200342229-001	Getty Images	Thinkstock
119	78526539	Comstock	Thinkstock
122	78376483	Jupiterimages, Brand X Pictures	Thinkstock
123	56570514	Stockbyte	Thinkstock
129	78290947	Goodshoot	Thinkstock
130	16875669	Candy Box Images	iStock
138	3243093	Hulton Archive	Getty Images
140	STK134103RKE	Stockbyte	Thinkstock
141	92847121	Photos.com	Thinkstock
145	110859556	The India Today Group	Getty Images
145	111718009	Sean Gallup	Getty Images
146	76754184	Creatas	Thinkstock
147	57614079	Stockbyte	Thinkstock
148	SKD182806SDC	George Doyle	Thinkstock
149	80402198	BananaStock	Thinkstock
149	DES_099	Stockbyte	Thinkstock
149	STK92512COR	George Doyle	Thinkstock
149	87750181	Zedcor Wholly Owned	Thinkstock
149	AA053796	Ryan VcVay	Thinkstock
150	200248653	Russell Illig	Thinkstock
151	SKD259377SDC	Stockbyte	Thinkstock
152	57340775	Stockbyte	Thinkstock
153	89693614	Jupiterimages	Thinkstock
154	92845973	Photos.com	Thinkstock
157	SPE_015	Stockbyte	Thinkstock
158	78320701	Brand X Pictures	Thinkstock
158	SB10066222NN-001	Erik Snyder	Thinkstock
166	90308506	Polka Dot RF	Thinkstock
169	87563546	Jupiterimages	Thinkstock
170	78368108	Jupiterimages	Thinkstock
171	87482935	Hamera Technologies	Thinkstock
172	87611714	Hemera Technologies	Thinkstock
173	2641930	Hulton Archive	Getty Images
175	Pareto Principle	Cohen Brown	Cohen Brown
176	Roy Rogers collage	Cohen Brown	Cohen Brown
177	Newspaper clipping	Used with permission	The Orlando Sentinel
178	87457782	Ablestock.com	Thinkstock
179	87539825	Jupiterimages	Thinkstock
180	97268258	RLRRLRLL	Shutterstock
181	78325415	Brand X Pictures	Thinkstock
183	116743908	Time & Life Pictures	Getty Images
184	200549067-001	Thomas Northcut	Thinkstock
186	15015281	Diego Cervo	iStock
188	200384172-001	John Rowley	Thinkstock
190	DV2171025	Digital Vision	Thinkstock
192	92830561	Photos.com	Thinkstock
193	SB10068701G	Donald Miralle	Thinkstock
194	57434804	Stockbyte	Thinkstock
204	86513558	Jupiterimages	Thinkstock
205	DV1922023	Digital Vision	Thinkstock
206	BU010162	Kevin Peterson	Thinkstock
208	87608307	Jupiterimages	Thinkstock
209	56676357	Medioimages/Photodisc	Thinkstock
210	78058311	Jupiterimages	Thinkstock
216	SKD181033SDC	George Doyle & Ciaran Griffin	Thinkstock
217	200288336-001	Ryan McVay	Thinkstock
219	MEDFR30035	Medioimages/Photodisc	Thinkstock
220	STK309038RKN	George Doyle	Thinkstock
223	9479052	Style-Photographs	iStock
224	SKD186791SDC	Stockbyte	Thinkstock
225	83313297	Michael Blann	Thinkstock
228	200488040	Siri Stafford	Thinkstock
229	80617596	Creatas	Thinkstock